Write 4 Today

Grade 2

Frank Schaffer Publications®

Editors: Kimberly Bradford, Linda Triemstra
Interior Design: Lori Kibbey

Frank Schaffer Publications®

Send all inquiries to:
Frank Schaffer Publications
3195 Wilson Drive NW
Grand Rapids, Michigan 49534

Write 4 Today—grade 2

ISBN: 0-7682-3222-8

2 3 4 5 6 7 8 9 10 PAT 10 09 08 07 06 05

Write 4 Today

Table of Contents

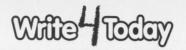

Introduction

Write 4 Today is a comprehensive yet quick and easy-to-use supplement sequenced to complement any second-grade writing curriculum. Essential writing skills and concepts are reviewed each day during a four-day period, with an evaluation each fifth day.

Unlike many writing programs, *Write 4 Today* is designed so that concepts are repeated weekly. This book supplies four concepts for four days covering a 40-week period. The focus alternates weekly between the mechanics of writing (capitalization, grammar, punctuation, and spelling) and the process of writing (prewriting/brainstorming, drafting, revising, and proofreading). A separate assessment is provided for the fifth day of each week.

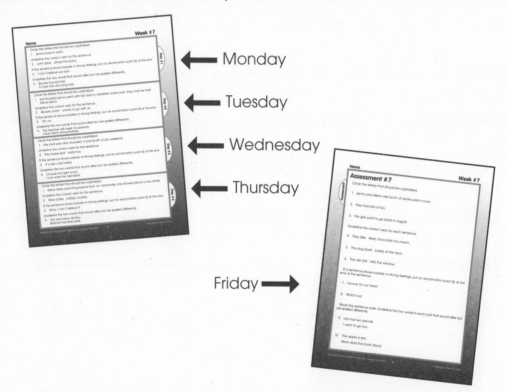

Because writing typically involves lengthier work than these short exercises require, many of the process exercises are ideal to use as springboards for more in-depth work. For example, if one task is creating an opening paragraph on a specific topic, the exercise could be expanded to include writing supporting paragraphs and a conclusion.

Answer keys are provided for daily drills and assessments (see pages 93–112). Concepts and skills are tested on an even/odd week rotation and follow a consistent format for ease of evaluation. Although the concepts and skills are individually categorized, most are interrelated so that many opportunities for practice and evaluation exist.

Write 4 Today was created in response to a need for ongoing practice after a skill had been addressed in the basal text. With the usual methods, a skill would be covered and then abandoned until it reappeared (sometimes) in a six-week cumulative review. With the growing emphasis on standardized testing, the necessity for experience with test styles and semantics also became apparent.

The daily approach of *Write 4 Today* provides risk-taking challenges, higher-level thinking exercises, problem-solving strategies, and necessary practice, emphasizing areas that frequently give students difficulty, such as punctuation and spelling. The program targets test-taking skills by incorporating the style and syntax of standardized tests.

For the even weeks, when the focus is on the writing process, use this ten-point rubic to assess the published work. You may cut and copy it onto the bottom of each assessment or attach it as a separate page. The rubric has been structured with a total of 10 possible points for each of the writing trait categories. These trait categories correlate with the popular 6 + 1 TRAITS* Writing Program (*a trademark of Northwest Regional Educational Laboratory) in this order from top to bottom: ideas, organization, voice, word choice, sentence fluency, conventions (covering all four COPS lines), and presentation. Use the rubric for student self assessments, or teacher assessments. Score the writing according to how often it clearly demonstrates each trait.

Never	Sometimes	Mostly	Always	**Grading Rubric**
1	4	7	10	**Focus** Writing sticks to the topic with focused main ideas and supporting details
1	4	7	10	**Order** Sentences and paragraphs have a clear order that makes sense to readers
1	4	7	10	**Tone** Words and sentences use an interesting tone of voice that fits the audience and the writing style
1	4	7	10	**Vocabulary** Writing uses a wide variety of vocabulary that is specific, accurate, strong, and original
1	4	7	10	**Flow** Sentences are easy to read and flow smoothly from one to the next
1	4	7	10	**Details** Capitalization is correct
1	4	7	10	Odd Grammar is corrected before publishing
1	4	7	10	Punctuation is correct
1	4	7	10	Spelling is correct
1	4	7	10	**Neatness** Writing is neat, clean, and easy to read

Writing Strategies

Choose a **topic** for your writing.
- What am I writing about?

Decide on a **purpose** for writing.
- Why am I writing this piece?
- What do I hope the audience will learn from reading this piece?

Identify your **audience**.
- Who am I writing to?

Decide on a writing **style**.
- Expository—gives information or explains facts or ideas
- Persuasive—tries to talk someone into something
- Narrative—tells a story
- Descriptive—presents a clear picture of a person, place, thing, or idea

Decide on a **genre**—essay, letter, poetry, autobiography, fiction, nonfiction.

Decide on a **point of view**—first person, second person, or third person.

Brainstorm by listing or drawing your main ideas.

Use a graphic organizer to organize your thoughts.

Revise, revise, revise!
- Use **descriptive words**.
- Use **transitions** and linking expressions.
- Use a **variety of sentence structures**.
- **Elaborate** with facts and details.
- Group your ideas into **paragraphs**.
- **Proofread** for capitalization, punctuation, and spelling.

Published by Frank Schaffer Publications. Copyright protected. 0-7682-3222-8 *Write 4 Today*

Idea Ball Planner

Directions: Label the sections. Write or draw ideas in each section.

0-7682-3222-8 *Write 4 Today*

Web Organizer

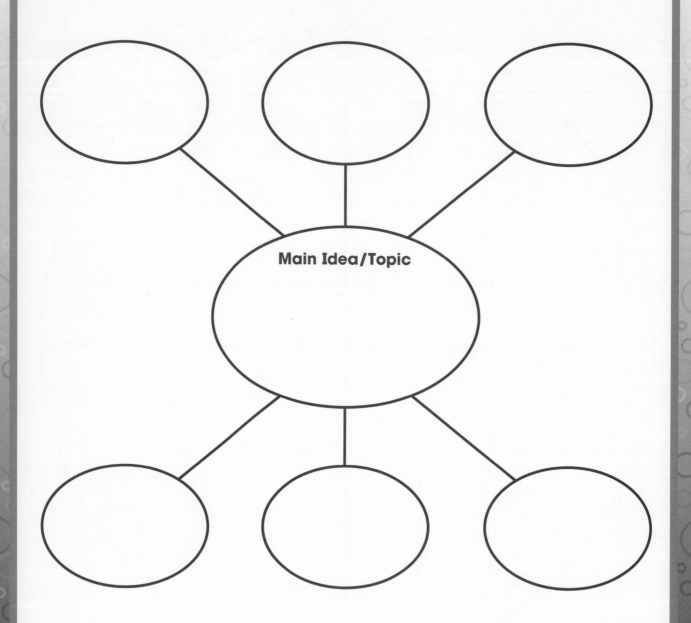

Main Idea/Topic

0-7682-3222-8 *Write 4 Today*

Five Ws Chart

Who?

What?

Why?

When?

Where?

Sequence Planner

Directions: Sometimes you write about a chain of events. You might also list the steps it takes to make something. Fill in the chart. List every event or step. List them in the order they happen.

Topic
First,
Next,
Then,
Next,
Then,
Finally,

0-7682-3222-8 *Write 4 Today*

Diagram Organizer

Directions: Complete this diagram for your topic.

Topic   Fact

Detail

Detail

Detail

Topic   Fact

Detail

Detail

Detail

Topic   Fact

Detail

Detail

Detail

Editing Checklist

Mechanics Checklist

☐ Every sentence begins with a capital letter and ends with the correct punctuation mark.

☐ Commas are in the right places.

☐ Words that need capital letters begin with capital letters.

☐ All words are spelled correctly.

☐ All sentences are one complete thought.

☐ There are no fragments or run-ons.

☐ The beginning of each paragraph is indented.

Style Checklist

☐ Verbs are interesting and exciting.

☐ Adjectives describe with detail. No boring words are used.

☐ Sentences show, not tell.

☐ The story has a beginning, a middle, and an end.

☐ Paragraphs have a topic sentence, supporting sentences, and a concluding sentence.

☐ Each sentence does not begin with the same word.

Proofreading Marks

¶ Indent a paragraph

∧ Insert something

⸜ Take something out

m̲̲ Capitalize

/ Make lowercase

Write the first word of the sentence with a capital letter.

1. (the) _____ flower smells very nice.

Circle the picture that has a short vowel sound. **Hint:** There may be more than one!

2.

Put a period at the end of the sentence if it tells something or gives a command.

3. Please sit down

Add an **s** to the noun to make it plural. Write the new word on the line.

4. bird _____

Day #1

Write the first word of the sentence with a capital letter.

1. (anne) _____ has a black kitten.

Circle the picture that has a short vowel sound. **Hint:** There may be more than one!

2.

Put a period at the end of the sentence if it tells something or gives a command.

3. John is tired

Add an **s** to the noun to make it plural. Write the new word on the line.

4. kitten _____

Day #2

Write the first word of the sentence with a capital letter.

1. (do) _____ you like to play baseball?

Circle the picture that has a short vowel sound. **Hint:** There may be more than one!

2.

Put a period at the end of the sentence if it tells something or gives a command.

3. Did you see your sister

Add an **s** to the noun to make it plural. Write the new word on the line.

4. tree _____

Day #3

Write the first word of the sentence with a capital letter.

1. (where) _____ is your pen?

Circle the picture that has a short vowel sound. **Hint:** There may be more than one!

2.

Put a period at the end of the sentence if it tells something or gives a command.

3. Eat your dinner

Add an **s** to the noun to make it plural. Write the new word on the line.

4. glove _____

Day #4

Assessment #1

Write the first word of the sentences with a capital letter.

1. (fruit) _____ is a good snack.

2. (turn) _____ on the light.

3. (blue) _____ is my favorite color.

Circle the pictures that have a short vowel sound.

4.

5.

Read the sentence. Put a period at the end of each sentence if it tells something or gives a command.

6. Why is Taylor running

7. That mouse ate all the cheese

8. My friends sang a birthday song

Add an **s** to the noun to make it plural. Write the new word on the line.

9. crayon _____

10. egg _____

prewrite/brainstorm

Look at the idea box. Write or draw your ideas in the box.

Pets	School
Toys	Family

draft

Use your ideas from the idea ball to finish the sentences.

1. My favorite pet is _____.

2. The toy I like the most is _____.

3. At school I _____.

4. I live with _____.

revise

Read the sentences you wrote. Can you make your sentences clearer? Rewrite each sentence.

_____

_____

_____

_____

proofread

It's time to proofread your sentences. Read them one more time. Do you see any capitalization errors? Are all the words spelled correctly? Did you use the correct punctuation and grammar? Use proofreading marks to correct the sentences.

- ❑ ✓ Capitalization Mistakes
- ❑ ✓ Odd Grammar
- ❑ ✓ Punctuation Mistakes
- ❑ ✓ Spelling Mistakes

Assessment # 2

publish

Now it is time to publish your writing. Write your final copy on the lines below.

MAKE SURE it turns out:

- NEAT—Make sure there are no wrinkles, creases, or holes.
- CLEAN—Erase any smudges or dirty spots.
- EASY TO READ—Use your best handwriting and good spacing between words.

_____

_____

_____

_____

_____

_____

_____

_____

_____

_____

_____

_____

_____

Use capital letters in titles. Rewrite the poem title using correct capitalization.

1.   "jack and jill" _____

Underline the nouns in the sentence. **Hint:** There may be none!

2.   Jeremy ate a sandwich.

If a sentence asks a question, put a question mark at the end of the sentence.

3.   Is the sandwich cold

Add an **e** to the word to make a new word. Write the new word on the lines.

4.   cut _____

Use capital letters in titles. Rewrite the magazine title using correct capitalization.

1.   *sports digest* _____

Underline the nouns in the sentence. **Hint:** There may be none!

2.   The rabbit is brown and white.

If a sentence asks a question, put a question mark at the end of the sentence.

3.   Is that your dog

Add an **e** to the word to make a new word. Write the new word on the lines.

4.   mop _____

Use capital letters in titles. Rewrite the book title using correct capitalization.

1.   *favorite tales* _____

Underline the nouns in the sentence. **Hint:** There may be none!

2.   Sit down!

If a sentence asks a question, put a question mark at the end of the sentence.

3.   Stop now

Add an **e** to the word to make a new word. Write the new word on the lines.

4.   can _____

Use capital letters in titles. Rewrite the book title using correct capitalization.

1.   *old yeller* _____

Underline the nouns in the sentence. **Hint:** There may be none!

2.   Where is your pencil?

If a sentence asks a question, put a question mark at the end of the sentence.

3.   Did you lose it

Add an **e** to the word to make a new word. Write the new word on the lines.

4.   pan _____

Assessment

Assessment #3

Use capital letters in titles. Rewrite the movie titles using correct capitalization.

1.

monsters, inc. _____

2.

cats and dogs _____

Underline the nouns in the sentences. **Hint:** There may be more than one or none!

3.   Roland is seven years old.

4.   Put the book away.

Read each sentence. If it asks a question, put a question mark at the end of the sentence.

5.   Who said that

6.   What is your name

7.   Maria is very smart

Add an **e** to each word to make a new word. Write the new word on the lines.

8.   bit _____

9.   tub _____

10. kit _____

prewrite/brainstorm

Fill in the character planner about a character from a story or one you have made up.

He/she hears: _____

He/she thinks about: _____

_____

He/she says: _____

He/she feels: _____

He/she likes to: _____

He/she goes to: _____

draft

Write four sentences about the character. Use ideas from your character planner.

_____

_____

_____

_____

revise

Read the sentences you wrote. Can you make your sentences clearer? Rewrite each sentence.

_____

_____

_____

_____

proofread

It's time to proofread your sentences. Read them one more time. Do you see any capitalization errors? Are all the words spelled correctly? Did you use the correct punctuation and grammar? Use proofreading marks to correct the sentences.

- ❑ ✓ Capitalization Mistakes
- ❑ ✓ Odd Grammar
- ❑ ✓ Punctuation Mistakes
- ❑ ✓ Spelling Mistakes

Assessment # 4

publish

Now it is time to publish your writing. Write your final copy on the lines below.

MAKE SURE it turns out:

- NEAT—Make sure there are no wrinkles, creases, or holes.
- CLEAN—Erase any smudges or dirty spots.
- EASY TO READ—Use your best handwriting and good spacing between words.

_____

_____

_____

_____

_____

_____

_____

_____

_____

_____

_____

_____

_____

Circle the letters that should be capitalized.

1. the science report is due monday.

Underline the verb in the sentence.

2. She hides under the bed.

Make up your own question. Remember to add a question mark at the end of the sentence.

3. Who _____

If a noun ends in *s*, *ss*, *sh*, *ch*, or *x*, add **es** to make it plural. Underline the letter or letters at the end of the word that tell you how to make the plural. Write the new word on the line.

4. glass _____

Circle the letters that should be capitalized.

1. tom's birthday is november 4.

Underline the verb in the sentence.

2. We eat pizza for lunch.

Make up your own question. Remember to add a question mark at the end of the sentence.

3. What _____

If a noun ends in *s*, *ss*, *sh*, *ch*, or *x*, add **es** to make it plural. Underline the letter or letters at the end of the word that tell you how to make the plural. Write the new word on the line.

4. match _____

Circle the letters that should be capitalized.

1. see dr. platt on wednesday.

Underline the verb in the sentence.

2. I swim on a team.

Make up your own question. Remember to add a question mark at the end of the sentence.

3. When _____

If a noun ends in *s*, *ss*, *sh*, *ch*, or *x*, add **es** to make it plural. Underline the letter or letters at the end of the word that tell you how to make the plural. Write the new word on the line.

4. gas _____

Circle the letters that should be capitalized.

1. soccer practice is changed to thursday.

Underline the verb in the sentence.

2. The bunny hops.

Make up your own question. Remember to add a question mark at the end of the sentence.

3. Where _____

If a noun ends in *s*, *ss*, *sh*, *ch*, or *x*, add **es** to make it plural. Underline the letter or letters at the end of the word that tell you how to make the plural. Write the new word on the line.

4. watch _____

Assessment # 5

Circle the letters that should be capitalized.

1. our pizza party is on saturday.

2. we always make crafts in november and december.

Underline the verb in the sentence.

3. Gina dances at school.

4. You laugh at everything!

5. Throw your trash in the bin.

Make up your own questions. Remember to add a question mark at the end of the sentence.

6. Why _____

7. How _____

If a noun ends in *s*, *ss*, *sh*, *ch*, or *x*, add **es** to make it plural. Underline the letter or letters at the end of the word that tell you how to make the plural. Write the new word on the line.

8. tax _____

9. brush _____

10. switch _____

Name

prewrite/brainstorm

Think of words that rhyme with *dot*.
Write them in the word web.

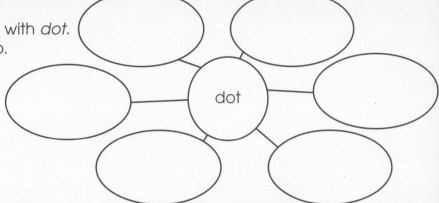

dot

draft

Write four silly sentences that rhyme. Use words from your rhyming word web.

_____

_____

_____

_____

revise

Read the rhyming sentences you wrote. Can you make your sentences clearer?
Rewrite each sentence.

_____

_____

_____

_____

proofread

It's time to proofread your rhyming sentences. Read them one more time. Do you
see any capitalization errors? Are all the words spelled correctly? Did you use the
correct punctuation and grammar? Use proofreading marks to correct the sentences.

- ❏ ✓ Capitalization Mistakes
- ❏ ✓ Odd Grammar
- ❏ ✓ Punctuation Mistakes
- ❏ ✓ Spelling Mistakes

Day #1

Day #2

Day #3

Day #4

0-7682-3222-8 *Write 4 Today*

Assessment #6

publish

Now it is time to publish your writing. Write your final copy on the lines below.

MAKE SURE it turns out:

- NEAT—Make sure there are no wrinkles, creases, or holes.
- CLEAN—Erase any smudges or dirty spots.
- EASY TO READ—Use your best handwriting and good spacing
  between words.

Name

Circle the letters that should be capitalized.

1. jenna loves to swim.

Underline the correct verb for the sentence.

2. John (play   plays) the piano.

If the sentence shows surprise or strong feelings, put an exclamation point (!) at the end.

3. I can't believe we won

Underline the two words that sound alike but are spelled differently.

4. Brooke has red hair.
    A hare has very long ears.

Circle the letters that should be capitalized.

1. last thursday jenna went with her dad to clarefield water park. they took her best friend elena.

Underline the correct verb for the sentence.

2. Beverly (want   wants) to go with us.

If the sentence shows surprise or strong feelings, put an exclamation point (!) at the end.

3. Oh, no

Underline the two words that sound alike but are spelled differently.

4. The teacher will meet my parents.
    I love meat and potatoes.

Circle the letters that should be capitalized.

1. the pool was very crowded. it was fourth of july weekend.

Underline the correct verb for the sentence.

2. The horses (eat   eats) hay.

If the sentence shows surprise or strong feelings, put an exclamation point (!) at the end.

3. It's very cold today

Underline the two words that sound alike but are spelled differently.

4. Choose the right word.
    I can write the alphabet.

Circle the letters that should be capitalized.

1. elena takes swimming lessons from mr. hernandez. she showed jenna a new stroke.

Underline the correct verb for the sentence.

2. Mae (bake   bakes) cookies.

If the sentence shows surprise or strong feelings, put an exclamation point (!) at the end.

3. Wow, I can't believe it

Underline the two words that sound alike but are spelled differently.

4. The wind blew all day.
    Brianne has blue eyes.

0-7682-3222-8 *Write 4 Today*

Assessment #7

Circle the letters that should be capitalized.

1. jenna and elena ate lunch at pirate pete's cove.

2. they had lots of fun.

3. the girls want to go back in august.

Underline the correct verb for each sentence.

4. They (like   likes) chocolate ice cream.

5. The dog (bark   barks) at the door.

6. The rain (hit   hits) the window.

If a sentence shows surprise or strong feelings, put an exclamation point (!) at the end of the sentence.

7. Hooray for our team

8. Watch out

Read the sentence pairs. Underline the two words in each pair that sound alike but are spelled differently.

9. Lita has two pencils.

    I want to go too.

10. The apple is red.

    Mom read the book aloud.

prewrite/brainstorm

How are fish and turtles alike? How are they different? Fill in the Venn diagram.

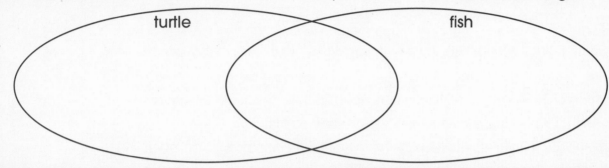

turtle   fish

draft

Write a few sentences that tell how a fish and a turtle are alike and different. Use your ideas from the diagram. Would you like a turtle or a fish for a pet? Why?

_____

_____

_____

_____

revise

Read the sentences you wrote. Can you make your sentences clearer? Rewrite each sentence.

_____

_____

_____

_____

proofread

It's time to proofread your sentences. Read them one more time. Do you see any capitalization errors? Are all the words spelled correctly? Did you use the correct punctuation and grammar? Use proofreading marks to correct the sentences.

❏ ✓ Capitalization Mistakes

❏ ✓ Odd Grammar

❏ ✓ Punctuation Mistakes

❏ ✓ Spelling Mistakes

Assessment #8

publish

Now it is time to publish your writing. Write your final copy on the lines below.

MAKE SURE it turns out:

- NEAT—Make sure there are no wrinkles, creases, or holes.
- CLEAN—Erase any smudges or dirty spots.
- EASY TO READ—Use your best handwriting and good spacing
   between words.

_____

_____

_____

_____

_____

_____

_____

_____

_____

_____

_____

_____

_____

Circle the letters that should be capitalized.

I.

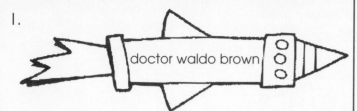

Write **C** next to the common nouns and **P** next to the proper nouns.

2. April _____   dog _____

Put the correct ending mark (**. ? !**) at the end of the sentence.

3. That bunny is so cute

Underline the word that is incorrect. Add a silent **e** to the word and write it on the line.

4. Staci at the crunchy apple.

_____

Day #1

Circle the letters that should be capitalized.

I.

Write **C** next to the common nouns and **P** next to the proper nouns.

2. Wednesday _____   Fifi _____

Put the correct ending mark (**. ? !**) at the end of the sentence.

3. Do you have a pet

Underline the word that is incorrect. Add a silent **e** to the word and write it on the line.

4. The clown gave Tom a candy can.

_____

Day #2

Circle the letters that should be capitalized.

I.

Write **C** next to the common nouns and **P** next to the proper nouns.

2. Pacific _____   lake _____

Put the correct ending mark (**. ? !**) at the end of the sentence.

3. My cat loves tuna fish

Underline the word that is incorrect. Add a silent **e** to the word and write it on the line.

4. I want to fly my kit.

_____

Day #3

Circle the letters that should be capitalized.

I.

Write **C** next to the common nouns and **P** next to the proper nouns.

2. boy _____   Italy _____

Put the correct ending mark (**. ? !**) at the end of the sentence.

3. I think turtles are fun

Underline the word that is incorrect. Add a silent **e** to the word and write it on the line.

4. Jared took car of his puppy.

_____

Day #4

Assessment #9

Assessment

Circle the letters that should be capitalized.

1.

uncle frederick

2.

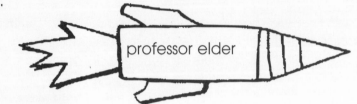

professor elder

3.

miss julia ames

Write **C** next to the common nouns and **P** next to the proper nouns.

4. Randi_____

5. flower _____

6. country_____

Put the correct ending mark (**. ? !**) at the end of each sentence.

7. Look at that

8. Have you ever seen a ferret

Underline the word that is incorrect. Add a silent **e** to the word and write it on the line.

9. Rip peaches are good to eat. _____

10. Mom wrote a not to my teacher. _____

prewrite/brainstorm

Fill in the chart. List facts and your opinions about the topic.

_____
Topic

Fact	Opinion

draft

Write a report about your topic. Use two facts and one opinion from the chart you completed.

_____

_____

_____

_____

revise

Read the sentences you wrote. Can you make your sentences clearer? Rewrite each sentence. Be sure to use specific nouns and verbs.

_____

_____

_____

_____

proofread

It's time to proofread your sentences. Read them one more time. Do you see any capitalization errors? Are all the words spelled correctly? Did you use the correct punctuation and grammar? Use proofreading marks to correct the sentences.

- ❏ ✓ Capitalization Mistakes
- ❏ ✓ Odd Grammar
- ❏ ✓ Punctuation Mistakes
- ❏ ✓ Spelling Mistakes

Assessment #10

publish

Now it is time to publish your writing. Write your final copy on the lines below.

MAKE SURE it turns out:

- NEAT—Make sure there are no wrinkles, creases, or holes.
- CLEAN—Erase any smudges or dirty spots.
- EASY TO READ—Use your best handwriting and good spacing between words.

Name

Underline the proper noun(s) that should begin with a capital letter. Write them correctly on the line.

1. I was born in new york city, new york. _____

Read the group of words. Circle the **S** if the words form a complete sentence. Circle the **F** if the words form a fragment.

2. S   F   The zoo is a fun place to go!

Use the words after the line to write a contraction to complete the sentence. Then put the correct mark (**. ! ?**) at the end of the sentence.

3. & 4. I _____ (can not) believe we won _____

Underline the proper noun(s) that should begin with a capital letter. Write them correctly on the line.

1. We live in orange county near the pacific ocean. _____

Read the group of words. Circle the **S** if the words form a complete sentence. Circle the **F** if the words form a fragment.

2. S   F   I love to see the snakes in the cages.

Use the words after the line to write a contraction to complete the sentence. Then put the correct mark (**. ! ?**) at the end of the sentence.

3. & 4. I _____ (do not) like this book _____

Underline the proper noun(s) that should begin with a capital letter. Write them correctly on the line.

1. lake superior is the largest lake in the united states. _____

Read the group of words. Circle the **S** if the words form a complete sentence. Circle the **F** if the words form a fragment.

2. S   F   into the alligator's pond

Use the words after the line to write a contraction to complete the sentence. Then put the correct mark (**. ! ?**) at the end of the sentence.

3. & 4. _____ (That is) nice _____

Underline the proper noun(s) that should begin with a capital letter. Write them correctly on the line.

1. chloe spent her summer at camp willow. _____

Read the group of words. Circle the **S** if the words form a complete sentence. Circle the **F** if the words form a fragment.

2. S   F   Will you carry the popcorn?

Use the words after the line to write a contraction to complete the sentence. Then put the correct mark (**. ! ?**) at the end of the sentence.

3. & 4. _____ (Do not) you want to keep it _____

Assessment #11

Underline the proper noun(s) that should begin with a capital letter. Write them correctly on the lines.

1. ted went to illinois and visited chicago. _____

   _____

2. bermuda is a country in the atlantic ocean. _____

   _____

3. The capital of michigan is lansing. _____

   _____

Read the groups of words. Circle the **S** if the words form a complete sentence. Circle the **F** if the words form a fragment.

4. S   F   the tall zookeeper

5. S   F   The lions are sleeping in the sun.

6. S   F   That seal splashed me!

Put the correct ending mark (**. ! ?**) at the end of the sentences.

7. Wow, it's just what I wanted

8. Why is this so cold

Read the sentences. Use the words under each line to write a contraction to complete the sentences.

9. I _____ think we will see Logan at the track meet.

   (do not)

10. Ryan says _____ his bike.

    (that is)

prewrite/brainstorm

Sometimes you write about a chain of events. Think about a chain of events. Fill in the chart. List every event. List them in the order they happen. If you need more room, write them on another paper.

Topic
First,
Next,
Then,
Next,
Then,
Finally,

draft

Read your list of events. Write a paragraph that contains all of the events.

_____

_____

_____

_____

revise

Read the paragraph you wrote. Did you put the events in the order they happened? Can you make your sentences clearer? Rewrite the paragraph. Be sure to use specific nouns and verbs.

_____

_____

_____

_____

proofread

It's time to proofread your paragraph. Read it one more time. Do you see any capitalization errors? Are all the words spelled correctly? Did you use the correct punctuation and grammar? Use proofreading marks to correct the sentences.

- ❏ ✓ Capitalization Mistakes
- ❏ ✓ Odd Grammar
- ❏ ✓ Punctuation Mistakes
- ❏ ✓ Spelling Mistakes

Assessment

Assessment #12

publish

Now it is time to publish your writing. Write your final copy on the lines below.

MAKE SURE it turns out:

- NEAT—Make sure there are no wrinkles, creases, or holes.
- CLEAN—Erase any smudges or dirty spots.
- EASY TO READ—Use your best handwriting and good spacing between words.

_____

_____

_____

_____

_____

_____

_____

_____

_____

_____

_____

_____

_____

_____

Read the song title. Rewrite the title with the correct capital letters.

1. "Mary had a little lamb" _____

Read the sentence. Circle the helping verb. Underline the main verb.

2. Next week I will sing in the school talent show.

Read the sentence. Add commas if they are needed.

3. My mother grows roses daisies and violets in her garden.

Write **your** or **you're** to correctly complete the sentence.

4. _____ invited to my sleepover.

Read the book title. Rewrite the title with the correct capital letters.

1. *the biography of helen keller* _____

Read the sentence. Circle the helping verb. Underline the main verb.

2. Someday I will teach my dog to fetch.

Read the sentence. Add commas if they are needed.

3. My brother's name is John Henry Mills.

Write **your** or **you're** to correctly complete the sentence.

4. Please bring _____ sleeping bag.

Read the magazine title. Rewrite the title with the correct capital letters.

1. *horse lover magazine* _____

Read the sentence. Circle the helping verb. Underline the main verb.

2. After school Carter can come to my house to play.

Read the sentence. Add commas if they are needed.

3. There are maple pine oak and elm trees on my street.

Write **your** or **you're** to correctly complete the sentence.

4. _____ welcome to bring your dog.

Read the book title. Rewrite the title with the correct capital letters.

1. *green eggs and ham* _____

Read the sentence. Circle the helping verb. Underline the main verb.

2. Jamal can watch the movie with me tonight.

Read the sentence. Add commas if they are needed.

3. We study spelling math history and art.

Write **your** or **you're** to correctly complete the sentence.

4. _____ mom will drive you to my house.

Assessment #13

Read the titles. Rewrite the titles with the correct capital letters.

1. "twinkle, twinkle, little star" _____

2. *the big book of lizards* _____

Read the sentences. Circle the helping verbs. Underline the main verbs.

3. Amy will write her report after class.

4. The bird can fly now that its wing is healed.

5. The sun will rise tomorrow.

Read the sentence. Add commas where they are needed.

6. Claire Phil Tammy Joe and I went to the movies together.

7. Tana brought a blanket food drinks and games to the park.

8. Mina's favorite colors are yellow purple blue and pink.

Write **your** or **you're** to correctly complete the sentences.

9. You have to call _____ parents.

10. _____ going to love my new video game!

prewrite/brainstorm

Joey loves ice cream.
His teacher wants to know
why he loves it. Help Joey
by filling out the idea sundae.

I Like Ice Cream

draft

Write a paragraph about why Joey loves ice cream. Use the ideas you put in the idea sundae.

_____

_____

_____

_____

revise

Read the paragraph you wrote. Did you use all of your ideas? Can you make your sentences clearer? Rewrite the paragraph. Be sure to use specific nouns and verbs.

_____

_____

_____

_____

proofread

It's time to proofread your paragraph. Read it one more time. Do you see any capitalization errors? Are all the words spelled correctly? Did you use the correct punctuation and grammar? Use proofreading marks to correct the sentences.

- ☐ ✓ Capitalization Mistakes
- ☐ ✓ Odd Grammar
- ☐ ✓ Punctuation Mistakes
- ☐ ✓ Spelling Mistakes

Day #1

Day #2

Day #3

Day #4

Assessment #14

publish

Now it is time to publish your writing. Write your final copy on the lines below.

MAKE SURE it turns out:

- NEAT—Make sure there are no wrinkles, creases, or holes.
- CLEAN—Erase any smudges or dirty spots.
- EASY TO READ—Use your best handwriting and good spacing between words.

_____

_____

_____

_____

_____

_____

_____

_____

_____

_____

_____

_____

Circle the correct verb. Use proofreading marks to show the correct capital letters.

1. & 2. my team (goes   go) to soccer practice on tuesdays and thursdays.

Read the sentence. Add apostrophes where they are needed.

3.   Jamals grass is thick and green.

Look at the picture. Circle the correct plural noun.

4.   monkeys   monkies

monkey

Circle the correct verb. Use proofreading marks to show the correct capital letters.

1. & 2. we (celebrate   celebrates) the fourth of july by boating on the lake.

Read the sentence. Add apostrophes where they are needed.

3.   One squirrels fur was soft and gray.

Look at the picture. Circle the correct plural noun.

4.   partys   parties

party

Circle the correct verb. Use proofreading marks to show the correct capital letters.

1. & 2. jenn's dance recital (are   is) in february on valentine's day.

Read the sentence. Add apostrophes where they are needed.

3.   The small dogs leash dragged on the ground as it ran.

Look at the picture. Circle the correct plural noun.

4.   babys   babies

baby

Circle the correct verb. Use proofreading marks to show the correct capital letters.

1. & 2. my sister (went   wents) to ellen's house on friday.

Read the sentence. Add apostrophes where they are needed.

3. The dogs owner ran behind the dog.

Look at the picture. Circle the correct plural noun.

4.   turkeys   turkies

turkey

Assessment

Assessment #15

Use proofreading marks to show the correct capital letters.

1. my sister will be six years old in may.

2. In january, we always go sledding on saturday mornings.

3. jamie's favorite holiday is hanukkah, which comes in december.

Circle the correct verb that completes each sentence.

4. Our team (wear   wears) red uniforms.

5. My grandparents (live   lives) next door.

Read the sentences. Add apostrophes where they are needed.

6. Jamies favorite dessert is ice cream.

7. The mother birds nest was made of mud and twigs.

8. My dads car is dark green.

Look at each picture. Circle the correct plural noun.

9.

valley

valleys   vallies

10.

story

storys   stories

prewrite/brainstorm

Look at the picture.
What are the kids doing?
Fill in the chart with the
five Ws about the picture.

Who?	What?	When?	Where?	Why?

draft

Write a paragraph about the picture. Use the five Ws from the chart.

_____

_____

_____

_____

revise

Read your paragraph about the picture. Did you include all five Ws? Are the words in the right order? Are your word groups sentences? Rewrite your paragraph.

_____

_____

_____

_____

proofread

Read your paragraph. Look at the words and see if they are spelled correctly. Did you capitalize the words that start each sentence? Use proofreading marks to correct your paragraph.

- ❏ ✓ Capitalization Mistakes
- ❏ ✓ Odd Grammar
- ❏ ✓ Punctuation Mistakes
- ❏ ✓ Spelling Mistakes

Assessment

Assessment #16

publish

Now it is time to publish your writing. Write your final copy on the lines below.
MAKE SURE it turns out:

- NEAT—Make sure there are no wrinkles, creases, or holes.
- CLEAN—Erase any smudges or dirty spots.
- EASY TO READ—Use your best handwriting and good spacing between words.

_____

_____

_____

_____

_____

_____

_____

_____

_____

_____

_____

_____

Use circles to show the incorrect capital letters.

1. my friends and i go to bear creek school.

If the group of words is a complete sentence, color the fish purple. If the group of words is not a sentence, color the fish green.

2. Fish eat worms.

Add quotation marks around what the person said.

3. Jill won a medal, yelled the coach.

Some words sound alike, but they have different meanings. Circle the word that best completes the sentence.

4. (Would   Wood) you like to meet my friend?

Use circles to show the incorrect capital letters.

1. byron has a dog named tilly and a cat named weed.

If the group of words is a complete sentence, color the fish purple. If the group of words is not a sentence, color the fish green.

2. at the bottom of the ocean

Add quotation marks around what the person said.

3. Todd said, I like dogs.

Some words sound alike, but they have different meanings. Circle the word that best completes the sentence.

4. Gail wore a (blew   blue) dress.

Use circles to show the incorrect capital letters.

1. my teacher is mrs. jamison.

If the group of words is a complete sentence, color the fish purple. If the group of words is not a sentence, color the fish green.

2. The whale lives in the deep water.

Add quotation marks around what the person said.

3. I'm going to walk to school, said Sue.

Some words sound alike, but they have different meanings. Circle the word that best completes the sentence.

4. My brother is (for   four) years old.

Use circles to show the incorrect capital letters.

1. jerry went to wyoming last year for Father's Day.

If the group of words is a complete sentence, color the fish purple. If the group of words is not a sentence, color the fish green.

2. swims along the rocky shore

Add quotation marks around what the person said.

3. Hit the ball! Bryan yelled at his little brother.

Some words sound alike, but they have different meanings. Circle the word that best completes the sentence.

4. The (sun   son) helps plants make food.

Day #1

Day #2

Day #3

Day #4

Assessment #17

Use circles to show the incorrect capital letters.

1. alicia read *the wind in the willows*.

2. aunt cindy is my favorite aunt.

3. brandon celebrates christmas with his grandparents.

Read each group of words. If it is a complete sentence, color the fish purple. If the group of words is not a sentence, color the fish green.

4. The ocean is very salty.

5. the great, white shark

Read the sentences. Underline the sentences that include a quote. Add quotation marks around what the person said.

6. I love apple pie, Emma told me.

7. You will like this story, Joey said.

Some words sound alike, but they have different meanings. Circle the word that best completes each sentence.

8. (Wood   Would) you like some ice cream?

9. We ate (blue   blew) jello for lunch.

10. I have (for   four) new pairs of shoes.

Day #1

prewrite/brainstorm

Do you know someone who deserves a "thank you"? Read the three ideas. Circle one that you like. To begin writing a thank-you letter, list three reasons why you want to say "thank you."

1. Thank you for the nice gift.

2. Thank you for being so nice.

3. Thank you for thinking of me.

3 Reasons

_____

_____

_____

Day #2

draft

Now it's time to write your thank-you letter. Write your letter to someone who deserves a "thank you." Use the format that is shown here. Be sure that you include the date and the person's name. At the end, sign your letter.

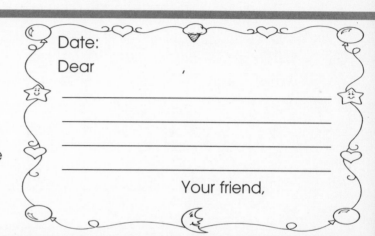

Date:

Dear _____ ,

_____

_____

_____

_____

Your friend,

Day #3

revise

After you write your letter, read it to make sure it says what you want it to say. Does the letter have the date? a friendly greeting? a thank you for something specific? Rewrite your letter with more specific words.

_____

_____

_____

_____

Day #4

proofread

Read your letter. Look at the words and see if they are spelled correctly. Did you capitalize the words that start each sentence? Use proofreading marks to correct your letter.

- ☐ ✓ Capitalization Mistakes
- ☐ ✓ Odd Grammar
- ☐ ✓ Punctuation Mistakes
- ☐ ✓ Spelling Mistakes

Assessment #18

publish

Now it is time to publish your writing. Write your final copy on the lines below.

MAKE SURE it turns out:

- NEAT—Make sure there are no wrinkles, creases, or holes.
- CLEAN—Erase any smudges or dirty spots.
- EASY TO READ—Use your best handwriting and good spacing between words.

_____

_____

_____

_____

_____

_____

_____

_____

_____

_____

_____

_____

Write **there**, **their**, or **they're** to correctly complete the sentence. Circle letters that should be capitalized.

1. & 2. it was _____ when i looked.

Use **or, and**, or **but** to join the sentences together. Use proofreading marks.

3. In his back yard, Juan found a cricket. Juan found a ladybug.

Read the envelope. Put commas in the right places.

4.
> It's a birthday party!
> Cassie Wyman
>
> Date: October 9 2002
>   423 Center Street
>
> Place: Pizza Paradise
>   Littleton Maine 89764

Write **there**, **their**, or **they're** to correctly complete the sentence. Circle letters that should be capitalized.

1. & 2. _____ french toast was tasty.

Use **or, and**, or **but** to join the sentences together. Use proofreading marks.

3. Britney likes math. Britney likes art.

Read the envelope. Put commas in the right places.

4.
> Cassie Wyman
>
> 423 Center Street
>
> Littleton Maine 89764

Write **there**, **their**, or **they're** to correctly complete the sentence. Circle letters that should be capitalized.

1. & 2. _____ students in mr. hsu's class.

Use **or, and**, or **but** to join the sentences together. Use proofreading marks.

3. We might have pizza for lunch. We might have salad for lunch.

Read the invitation. Put commas in the right places.

4.
> You're invited to a party!
> Lin Nance
>
> Date: January 23 2003
>   37 West Road
>
> Place: My house
>   Tampa Florida 62341

Write **there**, **their**, or **they're** to correctly complete the sentence. Circle letters that should be capitalized.

1. & 2. give _____ tickets to them.

Use **or, and**, or **but** to join the sentences together. Use proofreading marks.

3. I ran to school. I was late.

Read the envelope. Put commas in the right places.

4.
> Lin Nance
>
> 37 West Road
>
> Tampa Florida 62341

Assessment #19

Write **there**, **their**, or **they're** to correctly complete each sentence. Circle letters that should be capitalized.

1. & 2. i think _____ riding the roller coaster.

3. & 4. the roller coaster is over _____ by mrs. farmer.

5. & 6. We will go _____ and eat english muffins.

Read the sentence pairs. Use **or**, **and**, or **but** to join the sentences together. Use proofreading marks.

7. Dennis went to Ann's party. Tony went to Ann's party.

8. I saw you. I didn't hear what you said.

Read the invitation and envelope. Put commas in the right places.

9.

Boo! It's a Halloween party!
 Tyrone Hilliard
 	
 Date: October 31 2005
       10024 Wells Avenue
 	
 Place: My house
       Claremont California 91734

10.

	☐
Tyrone Hilliard 10024 Wells Avenue Claremont California 91734	

prewrite/brainstorm

Some people write stories about their lives. You can, too! Fill in the lines to begin your autobiography.

My name is _____

My favorite toy is _____

My favorite color is _____

I like to eat _____

My friends are _____

draft

Put your sentences in a paragraph. Make sure you put things in the order you want them to be said.

_____

_____

_____

_____

revise

Read your paragraph about yourself. Did you use all of your ideas? Can you make your sentences clearer? Rewrite the paragraph. Be sure to use specific nouns and verbs.

_____

_____

_____

proofread

Read your paragraph. Look at the words and see if they are spelled correctly. Did you capitalize the words that start each sentence? Use proofreading marks to correct your paragraph.

- ❐ ✓ Capitalization Mistakes
- ❐ ✓ Odd Grammar
- ❐ ✓ Punctuation Mistakes
- ❐ ✓ Spelling Mistakes

Assessment #20

publish

Now it is time to publish your writing. Write your final copy on the lines below.

MAKE SURE it turns out:

- NEAT—Make sure there are no wrinkles, creases, or holes.
- CLEAN—Erase any smudges or dirty spots.
- EASY TO READ—Use your best handwriting and good spacing
  between words.

_____

_____

_____

_____

_____

_____

_____

_____

_____

_____

_____

_____

_____

Use proofreading marks to show correct capital letters and punctuation at the end of the sentences.

1. & 2. linda had a birthday party How many people were at the party

Fill in the blank with **is** or **are**.

3. The children _____ putting on ice skates.

Read the sentence. If **to**, **too**, or **two** is used correctly, color the picture. If the word is used incorrectly, cross out the word and write the correct word above it.

4. Gabriel is going too catch the ball.

Use proofreading marks to show correct capital letters and punctuation at the end of the sentences.

1. & 2. bobby and maria came to the party They live across the street

Fill in the blank with **is** or **are**.

3. Andy _____ already skating.

Read the sentence. If **to**, **too**, or **two** is used correctly, color the picture. If the word is used incorrectly, cross out the word and write the correct word above it.

4. It is too windy to go outside.

Use proofreading marks to show correct capital letters and punctuation at the end of the sentences.

1. & 2. maria gomez gave linda a doll The doll had a yellow hat

Fill in the blank with **is** or **are**.

3. "You _____ skating fast," said the children.

Read the sentence. If **to**, **too**, or **two** is used correctly, color the picture. If the word is used incorrectly, cross out the word and write the correct word above it.

4. There are two frogs in the pond.

Use proofreading marks to show correct capital letters and punctuation at the end of the sentences.

1. & 2. bobby tucker gave her a book What is the book about

Fill in the blank with **is** or **are**.

3. Tia _____ skating too.

Read the sentence. If **to**, **too**, or **two** is used correctly, color the picture. If the word is used incorrectly, cross out the word and write the correct word above it.

4. Monkeys love two eat bananas.

Assessment #21

Rewrite each sentence with the correct capital letters and punctuation.

1. Did linda have a big birthday cake

   _____

2. john gave his sister warm mittens

   _____

3. Was jamie at the birthday party

   _____

4. linda had a fun party

   _____

Fill in the blanks with **is** or **are**.

5. The children _____ ready.

6. They _____ too.

7. Andy _____ getting tired.

Read each sentence. If **to**, **too**, or **two** is used incorrectly, cross it out and write the correct word above it.

8. To birds sang.

9. Harry went too the zoo.

10. I am going to school.

prewrite/brainstorm

Describing an object is easy if you have a plan. You can make a plan by writing your ideas in an idea web like the one below. Write the ideas from the web into the outline.

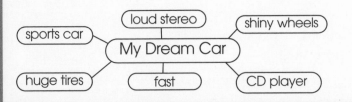

1. topic sentence: It has always been my dream to own a cool sports car.

2. a. one idea: _____

3. a. another idea: _____

4. a. last idea: _____

5. concluding idea: When I grow up, I'll buy a car like this.

draft

Put your sentences about the dream car in a paragraph. Make sure you put things in the order you want them to be said. Put related ideas together.

_____

_____

_____

_____

revise

Read your paragraph about the dream car. Did you use all of your ideas? Can you make your sentences clearer? Rewrite the paragraph. Be sure to use specific nouns and verbs.

_____

_____

_____

_____

proofread

Read your paragraph. Look at the words and see if they are spelled correctly. Did you capitalize the words that start each sentence? Use proofreading marks to correct your paragraph.

❏ ✓ Capitalization Mistakes

❏ ✓ Odd Grammar

❏ ✓ Punctuation Mistakes

❏ ✓ Spelling Mistakes

Day #1

Day #2

Day #3

Day #4

Assessment # 22

publish

Now it is time to publish your writing. Write your final copy on the lines below.

MAKE SURE it turns out:

- NEAT—Make sure there are no wrinkles, creases, or holes.
- CLEAN—Erase any smudges or dirty spots.
- EASY TO READ—Use your best handwriting and good spacing between words.

_____

_____

_____

_____

_____

_____

_____

_____

_____

_____

_____

_____

Fill in the blank with the correct contraction.

1. "We _____ going to paint now," said the teacher. (isn't, aren't)

Put quotation marks around the words the person said. Use proofreading marks to show capital letters.

2. & 3. karen rode her bike on walnut street. I'm bored, she said.

Read each noun. Write its plural.

4. rose _____   bee _____

Fill in the blank with the correct contraction.

1. The children _____ happy. (wasn't, weren't)

Put quotation marks around the words the person said. Use proofreading marks to show capital letters.

2. & 3. She visited nancy on central boulevard. Nancy said, Let's meet keisha.

Read each noun. Write its plural.

4. poppy _____   fly _____

Fill in the blank with the correct contraction.

1. "You _____ going to paint because you are going to the park," said the teacher. (isn't, aren't)

Put quotation marks around the words the person said. Use proofreading marks to show capital letters.

2. & 3. karen and nancy rode to garden avenue. Shall we play at our school? asked Keisha.

Read each noun. Write its plural.

4. bag _____   poem _____

Fill in the blank with the correct contraction.

1. The park _____ crowded today. (isn't, aren't)

Put quotation marks around the words the person said. Use proofreading marks to show capital letters.

2. & 3. They rode to their school on cherry road. Let's race! yelled the girls.

Read each noun. Write its plural.

4. box _____   wish _____

Assessment # 23

Assessment

Fill in the blanks with the correct contraction.

1. Amy still _____ happy. (wasn't, weren't)

2. "Why _____ you happy, Amy?" asked the teacher.
   (wasn't, weren't)

3. "I am unhappy because we _____ going to paint now," said Amy.
   (isn't, aren't)

Rewrite each sentence. Begin the names of streets with capital letters.

4. They passed apple road on their way.

   _____

5. Karen, Nancy, and Keisha crossed seventh street.

   _____

Put quotation marks around the words each person said. **Hint:** Periods, commas,
question marks, and exclamation points go inside quotation marks.

6. Did you read that book? asked Luisa.

7. Yes, said Becca. Did you?

Read each noun. Write its plural.

8. whale _____   tree _____

9. penny _____   sky _____

10. fox _____   bush _____

prewrite/brainstorm

Brainstorming is a way to think of all kinds of writing ideas. You might use some ideas. You might throw some out. Answer the questions below about your family.

How many people are in your family? _____

What are their names? _____

Write two words that tell about each person in your family.

_____

Do you have any pets? _____

What is your family's favorite thing to do together? _____

Day #1

draft

Use your answers to write five sentences about your family. Make sure you put things in the order you want them to be said. Put related ideas together.

_____

_____

_____

_____

Day #2

revise

Read your five sentences about your family. Do you want to change the order? Can you make your sentences clearer? Rewrite the sentences. Be sure to use specific nouns and verbs.

_____

_____

_____

_____

Day #3

proofread

Read your sentences about your family. Look at the words and see if they are spelled correctly. Did you capitalize the words that start each sentence? Use proofreading marks to correct your sentences.

- ❑ ✓ Capitalization Mistakes
- ❑ ✓ Odd Grammar
- ❑ ✓ Punctuation Mistakes
- ❑ ✓ Spelling Mistakes

Day #4

Assessment # 24

publish

Now it is time to publish your writing. Write your final copy on the lines below.

MAKE SURE it turns out:

- NEAT—Make sure there are no wrinkles, creases, or holes.
- CLEAN—Erase any smudges or dirty spots.
- EASY TO READ—Use your best handwriting and good spacing between words.

_____

_____

_____

_____

_____

_____

_____

_____

_____

_____

_____

_____

_____

Verbs that tell about the past that do not end with **-ed** are called irregular verbs. Read the sentence. Fill in the circle beside the verb form that tells what happened in the past.

1. ○ sees   ○ saw

Correct the punctuation and capitalization in the sentence.

2. & 3. manolo put paper a pencil an eraser and markers on his desk

Homophones are words that sound exactly the same, but they are spelled differently and mean different things. Write a sentence using the homophones below.

4. night knight _____

Verbs that tell about the past that do not end with **-ed** are called irregular verbs. Read the sentence. Fill in the circle beside the verb form that tells what happened in the past.

1. ○ wrote   ○ writes

Correct the punctuation and capitalization in the sentence.

2. & 3. manolo was ready to start his report on abraham lincoln

Write a sentence using the homophones below.

4. read red _____

Verbs that tell about the past that do not end with **-ed** are called irregular verbs. Read the sentence. Fill in the circle beside the verb form that tells what happened in the past.

1. ○ eat   ○ ate

Correct the punctuation and capitalization in the sentence.

2. & 3. Manolo said "the date was february 16 1809"

Write a sentence using the homophones below.

4. hour our _____

Verbs that tell about the past that do not end with **-ed** are called irregular verbs. Read the sentence. Fill in the circle beside the verb form that tells what happened in the past.

1. ○ did   ○ do

Correct the punctuation and capitalization in the sentence.

2. & 3. "That is when president lincoln was born, he said to his cat

Write a sentence using the homophones below.

4. see sea _____

Assessment #25

Assessment

Verbs that tell about the past that do not end with **-ed** are called irregular verbs. Read the sentence. Fill in the circle beside the verb form that tells what happened in the past.

1. ○ give   ○ gave

2. ○ took   ○ take

Correct the punctuation and capitalization in each sentence.

3. & 4. manolo said "Would you like to learn more about abraham lincoln

5. & 6. his cat purred and purred

7. & 8. okay, back to work," manolo said

Write a sentence using each pair of homophones below.

9. night   hour   _____

                        _____

10. knight   our   _____

                        _____

prewrite/brainstorm

How would your neighborhood be different if a dinosaur lived next door? Use the word web to think of ideas.

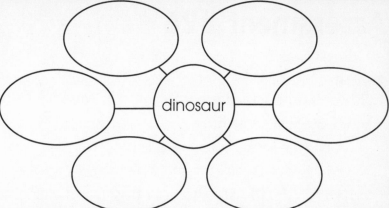

draft

Write two good things and two bad things about a dinosaur living next door. Write four sentences. Use ideas from your word web.

_____

_____

_____

_____

revise

Read your four sentences. Do you want to change the order? Can you make your sentences clearer? Rewrite the sentences. Be sure to use specific nouns and verbs.

_____

_____

_____

_____

proofread

Read your sentences one more time. Look at the words and see if they are spelled correctly. Did you capitalize the words that start each sentence? Use proofreading marks to correct your sentences.

- ❑ ✓ Capitalization Mistakes
- ❑ ✓ Odd Grammar
- ❑ ✓ Punctuation Mistakes
- ❑ ✓ Spelling Mistakes

Assessment #26

publish

Now it is time to publish your writing. Write your final copy on the lines below.

MAKE SURE it turns out:

- NEAT—Make sure there are no wrinkles, creases, or holes.
- CLEAN—Erase any smudges or dirty spots.
- EASY TO READ—Use your best handwriting and good spacing
  between words.

_____

_____

_____

_____

_____

_____

_____

_____

_____

_____

_____

_____

_____

Use proofreading marks or circles to show capital letters in the right places.
1. alice went to visit her grandma.

Fill in the blank with **saw** or **seen**.
2. Andy and Jim _____ Karl.

Put at least three items in a list. Remember to use commas.
3. My favorite foods are _____.

Change the singular noun to show ownership.
4. Tim _____

Use proofreading marks or circles to show capital letters in the right places.
1. She took her pet rabbit, fluffy.

Fill in the blank with **saw** or **seen**.
2. Karl _____ the boys in the park.

Put at least three items in a list. Remember to use commas.
3. I like the sports _____.

Change the singular noun to show ownership.
4. dog _____

Use proofreading marks or circles to show capital letters in the right places.
1. alice gave grandma adams a big hug.

Fill in the blank with **saw** or **seen**.
2. Andy and Jim already had _____ David and Fred.

Put at least three items in a list. Remember to use commas.
3. My favorite animals are _____.

Change the singular noun to show ownership.
4. mountain _____

Use proofreading marks or circles to show capital letters in the right places.
1. "where will i sleep?" asked alice.

Fill in the blank with **saw** or **seen**.
2. "Have you _____ David and Fred?" asked Karl.

Put at least three items in a list. Remember to use commas.
3. When I go on vacation, I take _____.

Change the singular noun to show ownership.
4. girl _____

Assessment #27

Use proofreading marks or circles to show capital letters in the right places.

1. "i have a nice room for you," said grandma.

2. "may fluffy sleep in my room?" asked alice.

3. "fluffy has her own bed outside," said grandma.

Fill in the blank with **saw** or **seen**.

4. "Yes, we _____ them playing ball," said Jim.

5. The boys _____ David and Fred.

6. "Have you _____ my new baseball?" asked Fred.

Put at least three items in a list. Remember to use commas.

7. When I go to school, I wear _____

8. I like the games _____

Change the singular nouns to show ownership.

9. desk _____   boy _____

10. lion _____   horse _____

prewrite/brainstorm

What do you think of when you think of fall? Leaves? Cider? Apples? Cold weather? Draw a picture in the box of your favorite fall activity.

draft

Look at the picture you drew. How can you describe it? Write a paragraph about what you like to do in the fall.

_____

_____

_____

_____

revise

Read your paragraph about what you like to do in the fall. Can you use different words? Do you want to change the order of ideas? Rewrite the sentences. Be sure to use specific nouns and verbs.

_____

_____

_____

_____

proofread

Read your paragraph one more time. Look at the words and see if they are spelled correctly. Did you capitalize the words that start each sentence? Use proofreading marks to correct your sentences.

- ☐ ✓ Capitalization Mistakes
- ☐ ✓ Odd Grammar
- ☐ ✓ Punctuation Mistakes
- ☐ ✓ Spelling Mistakes

Assessment #28

publish

Now it is time to publish your writing. Write your final copy on the lines below.

MAKE SURE it turns out:

- NEAT—Make sure there are no wrinkles, creases, or holes.
- CLEAN—Erase any smudges or dirty spots.
- EASY TO READ—Use your best handwriting and good spacing
  between words.

_____

_____

_____

_____

_____

_____

_____

_____

_____

_____

_____

_____

Use proofreading marks or circles to correct the capitalization in the sentence.

1. my brother and i attend palmview school on palm street.

Fill in the blank with **good** or **well**.

2. Will you teach me _____ gardening tricks?

Put commas in the right places.

3. There are many Danish bakeries in Solvang California.

Change the plural noun to make it possessive.

4. houses _____   boys _____

Use proofreading marks or circles to correct the capitalization in the sentence.

1. we have lived in hallandale, florida, since june 2000.

Fill in the blank with **good** or **well**.

2. I will teach you to garden _____ .

Put commas in the right places.

3. The new restaurant is located at 767 Stone Street Dallas Texas.

Change the plural noun to make it possessive.

4. lakes _____   tigers _____

Use proofreading marks or circles to correct the capitalization in the sentence.

1. who wrote the story titled "the loneliest girl in the world"?

Fill in the blank with **good** or **well**.

2. Use the _____ hose to water the garden.

Put commas in the right places.

3. My grandfather was born in October 1948 in Sante Fe New Mexico.

Change the plural noun to make it possessive.

4. cups _____   fathers _____

Use proofreading marks or circles to correct the capitalization in the sentence.

1. my dog, anabell, is the only pet i own.

Fill in the blank with **good** or **well**.

2. The plants are growing _____ .

Put commas in the right places.

3. Nancy bought lavender green yellow and pink wallpaper.

Change the plural noun to make it possessive.

4. girls _____   kittens _____

Assessment #29

Use proofreading marks or circles to correct the capitalization in the sentence.

1. have you ever gone to rocky mountain school?

2. will your mother be home soon?

3. "the mystery of black lake" is my favorite story.

Fill in the blank with **good** or **well**.

5. It is important to water the plants _____ .

6. Do radish leaves taste _____ ?

7. The leaves of many plants are _____ to eat.

Put commas in the right places.

5. Mother is making meat loaf baked potatoes and green beans for dinner.

6. It did not rain in Sacramento California in July 1980.

Change the plural noun to make it possessive.

9. mountains _____   pets _____

10. aunts _____   uncles _____

prewrite/brainstorm

The topic sentence in a paragraph tells the main idea. The supporting sentences explain more about the main idea. Think about this main idea: Ways that schools could recycle. Is recycling a good idea? Is it easy? Write **Recycle** in the big oval. On the lines, write three ideas about ways that schools could recycle.

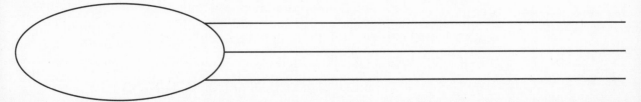

draft

Write a paragraph about ways that schools could recycle. For your first sentence, write: **Schools can recycle in three ways.** Next, use your three ideas to write three sentences that support the main idea.

_____

_____

_____

_____

revise

Now it's time to look at your paragraph and see how you can make it better. Do you have one main idea? Do your sentences support your main idea? Are the words in the right order? Are your word groups sentences? Rewrite your paragraph.

_____

_____

_____

_____

proofread

Read your paragraph one more time. Are the words spelled correctly? Did you capitalize the words that should start with a capital letter? Is the punctuation correct? Use proofreading marks to correct your paragraph.

- ❐ ✓ Capitalization Mistakes
- ❐ ✓ Odd Grammar
- ❐ ✓ Punctuation Mistakes
- ❐ ✓ Spelling Mistakes

Assessment # 30

publish

Now it is time to publish your writing. Write your final copy on the lines below.

MAKE SURE it turns out:

- NEAT—Make sure there are no wrinkles, creases, or holes.
- CLEAN—Erase any smudges or dirty spots.
- EASY TO READ—Use your best handwriting and good spacing between words.

_____

_____

_____

_____

_____

_____

_____

_____

_____

_____

_____

_____

_____

Draw a line under the correct group of words that begin the sentence.

1. (Mike and I   I and Mike)   took our kites to the park.

Put quotation marks where they belong in the sentence. Use proofreading marks to correct capitalization.

2. & 3. Ellen, mrs. Petersen is here to give you Piano lessons, said Mother.

See how many words you can put together to make compound words.

4. bath, room, bed, blue, bird (4 new words) _____

_____

Draw a line under the correct group of words that end the sentence.

1. Father came with   (Mike and me   me and Mike).

Put quotation marks where they belong in the sentence. Use proofreading marks to correct capitalization.

2. & 3. Hello, Mrs. petersen, Said Ellen.

See how many words you can put together to make compound words.

4. sun, rise, light, flash, house, dog (5 new words) _____

_____

Draw a line under the correct group of words.

1. Father told   (me and Mike   Mike and me)   to run.

Put quotation marks where they belong in the sentence. Use proofreading marks to correct capitalization.

2. & 3. Mrs. peterson asked, have you practiced all Week?

See how many words you can put together to make compound words.

4. sand, box, car, bag, shoe (4 new words) _____

_____

Draw a line under the correct group of words that begin the sentence.

1. (I and Mike   Mike and I)   ran fast.

Put quotation marks where they belong in the sentence. Use proofreading marks to correct capitalization.

2. & 3. Yes, i have practiced thirty Minutes every day, said ellen.

See how many words you can put together to make compound words.

4. pan, cake, cup, tea, pot, flower (5 new words) _____

_____

Assessment #31

Draw a line under the correct group of words to complete each sentence.

1. (Mike and I   I and Mike)   flew the kites high.

2. (I and Mike   Mike and I)   were tired.

3. Father brought   (me and Mike   Mike and me)   a cold drink.

Put quotation marks where they belong in the sentence. Then use proofreading marks to show letters that should be capitalized.

4. & 5. wonderful! exclaimed mrs. Petersen.

6. & 7. What shall i play first? asked ellen.

8. & 9. i'd like to hear you practice the scale first, Said Mrs. petersen.

See how many words you can put together to make compound words.

10.   way, door, knob, hall, bell (4 new words)

_____

_____

prewrite/brainstorm

The topic sentence in a paragraph tells the main idea. The supporting sentences explain more about the main idea. Some supporting sentences give examples. Read the topic sentence below. Write three examples that support the main idea.

Ice cream is my favorite dessert for three reasons.

_____

_____

_____

draft

Write a paragraph. Begin with the topic sentence. Next, write your three examples that support the topic sentence.

_____

_____

_____

_____

revise

Revise your paragraph. Did you start with the main idea? Did you write three examples that support the main idea? Did you use specific words to describe your examples? Rewrite your paragraph and use specific words.

_____

_____

_____

_____

proofread

Read your paragraph one more time. Look at the words and see if they are spelled correctly. Did you capitalize the words that should start with a capital letter? Is the punctuation correct? Use proofreading marks to correct your paragraph.

- ☐ ✓ Capitalization Mistakes
- ☐ ✓ Odd Grammar
- ☐ ✓ Punctuation Mistakes
- ☐ ✓ Spelling Mistakes

Assessment #32

publish

Now it is time to publish your writing. Write your final copy on the lines below.

MAKE SURE it turns out:

- NEAT—Make sure there are no wrinkles, creases, or holes.
- CLEAN—Erase any smudges or dirty spots.
- EASY TO READ—Use your best handwriting and good spacing between words.

_____

_____

_____

_____

_____

_____

_____

_____

_____

_____

_____

_____

_____

Fill in the line with the correct verb.

1. The children _____ going to see a movie. (is, are)

Put commas, apostrophes, quotation marks, and capital letters where they belong.

2. & 3. lynns mother bought pink blue red and yellow ribbon.

Circle the correct plural form of the noun.

4. dishs   dishes

Fill in the line with the correct verb.

1. Pete has _____ the movie. (saw, seen)

Put commas, apostrophes, quotation marks, and capital letters where they belong.

2. & 3. Gilbert wasnt that J. c. klein? asked Father.

Circle the correct plural form of the noun.

4. watches   watchs

Fill in the line with the correct verb.

1. "It _____ a good movie," said Pete. (is, are)

Put commas, apostrophes, quotation marks, and capital letters where they belong.

2. & 3. Oh what an exciting game! exclaimed uncle tim.

Circle the correct plural form of the noun.

4. bunnys   bunnies

Fill in the line with the correct verb.

1. The other children have not _____ it yet. (saw, seen)

Put commas, apostrophes, quotation marks, and capital letters where they belong.

2. & 3. Yes Beverly Ive seen fluffy today, said joan.

Circle the correct plural form of the noun.

4. men   mens

Assessment #33

Read the sentence. Draw three lines under any letters that should be capitalized.

1. The twins, matt and nick, threw their toys everywhere.

2. dr. ann s. sharp is my doctor.

Fill in the line with the correct verb.

3. Tim's mother _____ taking them to the movie. (is, are)

4. She has not _____ yet. (come, came)

5. The children _____ Tim's mother in the car. (saw, seen)

Put commas, apostrophes, and quotation marks where they belong in the sentence.

6. Why havent you finished the homework? asked Antwone.

7. Ive been to Lake Michigan Lake Erie and Lake Huron, said Karen.

8. The childs dog is lost.

Circle the correct plural form of the noun.

9. watches   watchs

10. mens   men

prewrite/brainstorm

A concluding sentence comes at the end of a paragraph. It tells the main idea in a different way, or it gives the reader something to think about. What is your favorite book? In the oval, write the title of your favorite book. On the three lines next to it, write three supporting ideas about why you like the book.

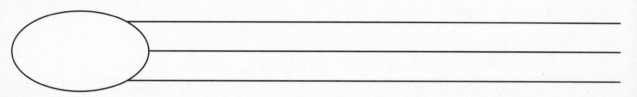

draft

Write a topic sentence about why you like your favorite book. Write three sentences supporting why you like the book. Now write a concluding sentence that tells your main idea in a different way.

_____

_____

_____

_____

revise

Read your paragraph. Did you name the book? Did you begin with a topic sentence? Did you write three supporting sentences to explain your main idea? Does your concluding statement tell your main idea in a different way? Rewrite your paragraph.

_____

_____

_____

_____

proofread

Read your paragraph one more time. Look at the words and see if they are spelled correctly. Did you capitalize the words that should start with a capital letter? Is the punctuation correct? Use proofreading marks to correct your paragraph.

- ❏ ✓ Capitalization Mistakes
- ❏ ✓ Odd Grammar
- ❏ ✓ Punctuation Mistakes
- ❏ ✓ Spelling Mistakes

Assessment

Assessment #34

publish

Now it is time to publish your writing. Write your final copy on the lines below.

MAKE SURE it turns out:

- NEAT—Make sure there are no wrinkles, creases, or holes.
- CLEAN—Erase any smudges or dirty spots.
- EASY TO READ—Use your best handwriting and good spacing between words.

_____

_____

_____

_____

_____

_____

_____

_____

_____

_____

_____

_____

_____

Use proofreading marks to correct the capitalization error. Add quotation marks.

1. & 2. what does the news say about school? asked Maya.

Write **statement**, **question**, **exclamation**, or **command** on the line to name the type of sentence.

3. "There is no school today," her mother replied. _____

Use proofreading marks to correct the spelling error in the sentence.

4. Jason is goeing to play in the snow.

Use proofreading marks to correct the capitalization error. Add quotation marks.

1. & 2. Johanna wanted to know, can we play in the snow?

Write **statement**, **question**, **exclamation**, or **command** on the line to name the type of sentence.

3. "You may play outside after you get dressed," said her mother. _____

Use proofreading marks to correct the spelling error in the sentence.

4. "Your gloves are on the shelf," said Mom, "or mabey in the closet."

Use proofreading marks to correct the capitalization error. Add quotation marks.

1. & 2. are you going to build a snowman today? asked Dad.

Write **statement**, **question**, **exclamation**, or **command** on the line to name the type of sentence.

3. "Let's go!" _____

Use proofreading marks to correct the spelling error in the sentence.

4. "I found my gloves. But were are my boots?" Maya asked.

Use proofreading marks to correct the capitalization error. Add quotation marks.

1. & 2. Maya asked, do you think Jason and Karl will go outside in the snow, too?

Write **statement**, **question**, **exclamation**, or **command** on the line to name the type of sentence.

3. "Call them on the phone and find out." _____

Use proofreading marks to correct the spelling error in the sentence.

4. "I'm ready too go now!" Karl yelled.

Assessment

Assessment #35

Read the sentences. Use proofreading marks to correct the capitalization errors.

1.   "i'm ready, too," said Jason.

2.   "mom, will you make hot chocolate for us when we come back?" Karl said.

Write **statement**, **question**, **exclamation**, or **command** on the lines to name the types of sentences.

3.   "How long will you be outside?" _____

4.   "I don't know." _____

5.   "Wow!" _____

Quotation marks are missing from the sentences. Add the quotation marks.

6.   Hey! Don't throw snowballs at me, Maya hollered.

7.   Karl said, Let's build a snowman and make snow angels.

Use proofreading marks to correct the spelling errors in the sentences.

8.   "Who is goning to throw that snowball?"

9.   "Do you think it is to cold outside to play?"

10.   "Mabye I am ready for my hot chocolate now."

prewrite/brainstorm

An informative paragraph gives information. Use the word web to write information about your family. Write **my family** on the line in the big circle. Write your ideas about your family in the ovals.

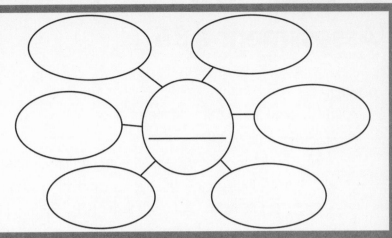

draft

Now it's time to write an informative paragraph about your family. Start with the topic sentence **I have a special family**. Use your ideas from the word web. Write three supporting sentences and a concluding sentence.

_____

_____

_____

_____

revise

Look at your paragraph. Does it start with the topic sentence? Does it have at least three supporting sentences? Does it have a concluding sentence? Rewrite your paragraph.

_____

_____

_____

_____

proofread

Read your paragraph one more time. Look at the words and see if they are spelled correctly. Did you capitalize the words that should start with a capital letter? Is the punctuation correct? Use proofreading marks to correct your paragraph.

- ☐ ✓ Capitalization Mistakes
- ☐ ✓ Odd Grammar
- ☐ ✓ Punctuation Mistakes
- ☐ ✓ Spelling Mistakes

Day #1

Day #2

Day #3

Day #4

Assessment #36

publish

Now it is time to publish your writing. Write your final copy on the lines below.
MAKE SURE it turns out:

- NEAT—Make sure there are no wrinkles, creases, or holes.
- CLEAN—Erase any smudges or dirty spots.
- EASY TO READ—Use your best handwriting and good spacing between words.

_____

_____

_____

_____

_____

_____

_____

_____

_____

_____

_____

_____

_____

Name

Use proofreading marks to fix the capitalization and to add commas.

1. & 2. On november 5 1998 senator john Glenn went into space.

Put a check mark on the line if the sentence is a run-on. If it is a run-on, rewrite the sentence.

3. _____ The book I like best is *Little House on the Prairie*. _____

_____

Circle the choice that shows the right spelling of the word.

4. That shirt was really _____ !   a. cheyp   b. cheap   c. cheip

---

Use proofreading marks to fix the capitalization and to add commas.

1. & 2. John glenn the oldest Astronaut ever was 77 years old.

Put a check mark on the line if the sentence is a run-on. Rewrite the sentence to correct the run-on.

3. _____ The part where Laura and her whole family get sick is scary, I was scared.

_____

Circle the choice that shows the right spelling of the word.

4. The _____ is sweet and cold.   a. lemonaid   b. lemonade   c. lemanade

---

Use proofreading marks to fix the capitalization and to add commas.

1. & 2. This was not the first time john glenn was in Space our teacher told us.

Put a check mark on the line if the sentence is a run-on. Rewrite the sentence to correct the run-on.

3. _____ The best part of this book is the characters. _____

_____

Circle the choice that shows the right spelling of the word.

4. I have a necklace made with _____.   a. beed   b. beids   c. beads

---

Use proofreading marks to fix the capitalization and to add commas.

1. & 2. He was the first american to circle Earth in the mercury "friendship 7."

Put a check mark on the line if the sentence is a run-on. Rewrite the sentence to correct the run-on.

3. _____ Pa is wise Pa is kind. _____

_____

Circle the choice that shows the right spelling of the word.

4. I made a _____ for Valentine's Day.   a. heart   b. haert   c. hart

Assessment #37

Use proofreading marks to fix the capitalization and to add commas.

1. & 2. in 1998 John glenn went into Space with six other Astronauts.

3. & 4. They rode in the space shuttle "discovery" our teacher told us.

Put a check mark on the line if the sentence is a run-on. Rewrite the sentence to correct the run-on.

5. ____ Laura is smart and stubborn.

_____

6. ____ Mary is a know-it-all, she seems a lot like my big sister.

_____

7. ____ The author is Laura Ingalls Wilder she is a great author.

_____

Use proofreading marks to fix the spelling in these sentences.

8. I'm happy the food is cheape here.

9. The Valentine's hart I made in class is pink.

10. I have a necklace of red and blue beeds.

Name

prewrite/brainstorm

Narrative writing tells a story that may or may not be true. To plan a story, you use a story map. You need characters, a setting, and a problem. Next, you need events and a solution.

Here are your characters, setting, and problem: You and your best friend are at the beach on Saturday, and you find a bottle with a treasure map inside. You don't know if it's real or not. Write one event and a solution based on this information.

_____

_____

draft

Write a paragraph about you, your friend, and the treasure map you found on the beach. Describe the event that happens after you find the map. Write the solution to the story.

_____

_____

_____

_____

revise

Read your paragraph. Does it tell the story in the right order? Did you introduce your topic? Did you write a solution to the story? Rewrite your paragraph, and make your words more specific.

_____

_____

_____

_____

proofread

Now it's time to proofread your paragraph. Are all of the words spelled correctly? Did you capitalize words that need to be capitalized? Did you use the correct verbs and nouns? Proofread your paragraph.

- ❐ ✓ Capitalization Mistakes
- ❐ ✓ Odd Grammar
- ❐ ✓ Punctuation Mistakes
- ❐ ✓ Spelling Mistakes

Assessment #38

Assessment

publish

Now it is time to publish your writing. Write your final copy on the lines below.

MAKE SURE it turns out:

- NEAT—Make sure there are no wrinkles, creases, or holes.
- CLEAN—Erase any smudges or dirty spots.
- EASY TO READ—Use your best handwriting and good spacing between words.

_____

_____

_____

_____

_____

_____

_____

_____

_____

_____

_____

_____

_____

_____

Circle the choice that shows correct capitalization.

1. a. miguel is proud   b. that his Dad   c. runs the police department.

Fill in the blank with the correct word.

2. Sara and _____ are best friends. (I, me)

Put commas where they are needed in the sentence.

3. Edward Johnson was born on June 25 1998 in Frenchtown Montana.

On a separate piece of paper, write one sentence for each homophone.

4. buy (purchase)   bye (farewell)

Circle the choice that shows correct capitalization.

1. a. Ms. Teeter   b. has a Cousin   c. who is a Sioux Chief.

Fill in the blank with the correct word.

2. The boys did all the work _____ . (himself, herself, themselves)

Put commas where they are needed in the sentence.

3. Who lives at 1066 First Avenue Banning California?

On a separate piece of paper, write one sentence for each homophone.

4. chilly (cool)   chili (food)

Circle the choice that shows correct capitalization.

1. a. alyson wants   b. to take an Exam   c. to become a detective.

Fill in the blank with the correct word.

2. I like chocolate cake, _____ . (to, two, too)

Put commas where they are needed in the sentence.

3. Oh Richard and Stacy already bought apples pears and grapes at the market.

On a separate piece of paper, write one sentence for each homophone.

4. fir (tree)   fur (on an animal)

Circle the choice that shows correct capitalization.

1. a. My grandma Lives in b. Chicago, Illinois,   c. near michigan avenue.

Fill in the blank with the correct word.

2. Have you _____ your English homework? (did, done)

Put commas where they are needed in the sentence.

3. "Will you bring the book with you Patty?" asked Frank.

On a separate piece of paper, write one sentence for each homophone.

4. hair (on head)   hare (rabbit)

Assessment #39

Circle the choice that shows correct capitalization.

1. a. The city of pontiac

   b. was named for a Chief

   c. who lived in Michigan.

2. a. Mystic, connecticut

   b. is the Town where

   c. my grandparents live.

Fill in the blank with the correct word.

3. There are _____ many children swimming today. (to, two, too)

4. Luisa went to the movies by _____ . (himself, herself, themselves)

5. Joey and _____ ran to the store. (I, me)

Put commas where they are needed in the sentence.

6. "Oh I forgot the book at school," said Patty.

7. "Can we borrow another book Frank?" she asked.

Write one sentence for each homophone.

8. road (street) _____

   rode (from ride) _____

9. shoe (covers foot) _____

   shoo (chase away) _____

10. lay (recline) _____

    lei (flower necklace) _____

Assessment

prewrite/brainstorm

You have decided to enter the "Take a Family Vacation on Us" contest. To enter you must submit an eight-line poem which explains why your family should win the vacation. Use the idea web to organize your thoughts. You may add more boxes on a separate piece of paper.

Take a Vacation on Us Contest

Reasons My Family Deserves to Win	Adjectives That Describe My Family

draft

The winning poem must express good reasons for needing the vacation. Write your eight-line poem. Be sure to support your reasons with specific words.

_____

_____

_____

_____

revise

Read your poem. Does it tell the reasons your family should win the vacation? Did you use good words to describe your reasons? Did you write eight lines? Rewrite your poem, and make your words more specific.

_____

_____

_____

_____

proofread

Now it's time to proofread your poem. Are all of the words spelled correctly? Did you capitalize words that need to be capitalized? Did you use the correct verbs and nouns? Use proofreading marks to correct your poem.

- ❑ ✓ Capitalization Mistakes
- ❑ ✓ Odd Grammar
- ❑ ✓ Punctuation Mistakes
- ❑ ✓ Spelling Mistakes

Assessment

Assessment #40

publish

Now it is time to publish your writing. Write your final copy on the lines below.

MAKE SURE it turns out:

- NEAT—Make sure there are no wrinkles, creases, or holes.
- CLEAN—Erase any smudges or dirty spots.
- EASY TO READ—Use your best handwriting and good spacing between words.

_____

_____

_____

_____

_____

_____

_____

_____

_____

_____

_____

_____

_____

Answer Key

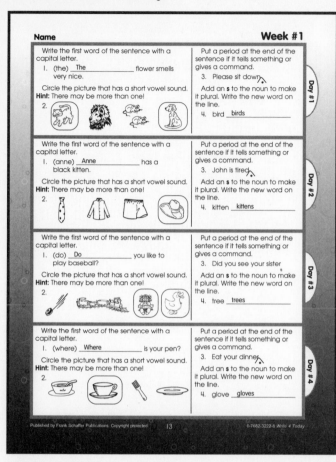

Name   Week #1

Day #1

Write the first word of the sentence with a capital letter.
1. (the) __The__ flower smells very nice.

Circle the picture that has a short vowel sound.
Hint: There may be more than one!
2.

Put a period at the end of the sentence if it tells something or gives a command.
3. Please sit down.

Add an **s** to the noun to make it plural. Write the new word on the line.
4. bird __birds__

Day #2

Write the first word of the sentence with a capital letter.
1. (anne) __Anne__ has a black kitten.

Circle the picture that has a short vowel sound.
Hint: There may be more than one!
2.

Put a period at the end of the sentence if it tells something or gives a command.
3. John is tired.

Add an **s** to the noun to make it plural. Write the new word on the line.
4. kitten __kittens__

Day #3

Write the first word of the sentence with a capital letter.
1. (do) __Do__ you like to play baseball?

Circle the picture that has a short vowel sound.
Hint: There may be more than one!
2.

Put a period at the end of the sentence if it tells something or gives a command.
3. Did you see your sister

Add an **s** to the noun to make it plural. Write the new word on the line.
4. tree __trees__

Day #4

Write the first word of the sentence with a capital letter.
1. (where) __Where__ is your pen?

Circle the picture that has a short vowel sound.
Hint: There may be more than one!
2.

Put a period at the end of the sentence if it tells something or gives a command.
3. Eat your dinner.

Add an **s** to the noun to make it plural. Write the new word on the line.
4. glove __gloves__

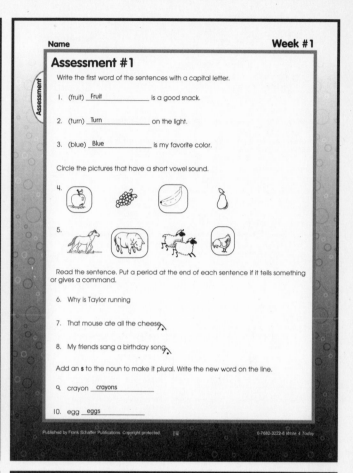

Name   Week #1

Assessment #1

Write the first word of the sentences with a capital letter.

1. (fruit) __Fruit__ is a good snack.

2. (turn) __Turn__ on the light.

3. (blue) __Blue__ is my favorite color.

Circle the pictures that have a short vowel sound.

4.

5.

Read the sentence. Put a period at the end of each sentence if it tells something or gives a command.

6. Why is Taylor running

7. That mouse ate all the cheese.

8. My friends sang a birthday song.

Add an **s** to the noun to make it plural. Write the new word on the line.

9. crayon __crayons__

10. egg __eggs__

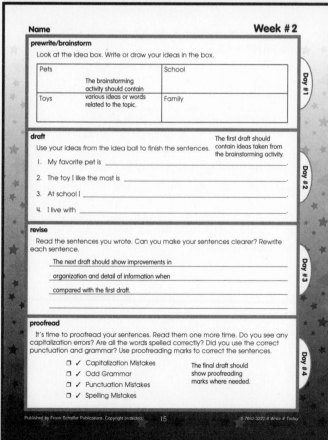

Name   Week #2

prewrite/brainstorm

Look at the idea box. Write or draw your ideas in the box.

Pets	The brainstorming activity should contain various ideas or words related to the topic.	School
Toys		Family

Day #1

draft

Use your ideas from the idea ball to finish the sentences.
1. My favorite pet is _____
2. The toy I like the most is _____
3. At school I _____
4. I live with _____

The first draft should contain ideas taken from the brainstorming activity.

Day #2

revise

Read the sentences you wrote. Can you make your sentences clearer? Rewrite each sentence.

The next draft should show improvements in organization and detail of information when compared with the first draft.

Day #3

proofread

It's time to proofread your sentences. Read them one more time. Do you see any capitalization errors? Are all the words spelled correctly? Did you use the correct punctuation and grammar? Use proofreading marks to correct the sentences.

☐ ✓ Capitalization Mistakes
☐ ✓ Odd Grammar
☐ ✓ Punctuation Mistakes
☐ ✓ Spelling Mistakes

The final draft should show proofreading marks where needed.

Day #4

Name   Week #2

Assessment #2

publish

Now it is time to publish your writing. Write your final copy on the lines below.
MAKE SURE it turns out:
- NEAT—Make sure there are no wrinkles, creases, or holes.
- CLEAN—Erase any smudges or dirty spots.
- EASY TO READ—Use your best handwriting and good spacing between words.

The content of writing samples will vary. Check to be sure that students have correctly completed all of the earlier steps in the writing process and have followed instructions for publishing their work. Use rubic on page 5 to assess.

Answer Key

Use capital letters in titles. Rewrite the poem title using correct capitalization.
1. "jack and jill"   "Jack and Jill"

Underline the nouns in the sentence. **Hint:** There may be none!
2. <u>Jeremy</u> ate a <u>sandwich</u>.

If a sentence asks a question, put a question mark at the end of the sentence.
3. Is the sandwich cold?

Add an **e** to the word to make a new word. Write the new word on the lines.
4. cut <u>cute</u>

Day #1

Use capital letters in titles. Rewrite the magazine title using correct capitalization.
1. sports digest   Sports Digest

Underline the nouns in the sentence. **Hint:** There may be none!
2. The <u>rabbit</u> is brown and white.

If a sentence asks a question, put a question mark at the end of the sentence.
3. Is that your dog?

Add an **e** to the word to make a new word. Write the new word on the lines.
4. mop <u>mope</u>

Day #2

Use capital letters in titles. Rewrite the book title using correct capitalization.
1. favorite tales   Favorite Tales

Underline the nouns in the sentence. **Hint:** There may be none!
2. Sit down!

If a sentence asks a question, put a question mark at the end of the sentence.
3. Stop now

Add an **e** to the word to make a new word. Write the new word on the lines.
4. can <u>cane</u>

Day #3

Use capital letters in titles. Rewrite the book title using correct capitalization.
1. old yeller   Old Yeller

Underline the nouns in the sentence. **Hint:** There may be none!
2. Where is your <u>pencil</u>?

If a sentence asks a question, put a question mark at the end of the sentence.
3. Did you lose it?

Add an **e** to the word to make a new word. Write the new word on the lines.
4. pan <u>pane</u>

Day #4

Assessment #3

Use capital letters in titles. Rewrite the movie titles using correct capitalization.

1. monsters, inc.   Monsters, Inc.

2. cats and dogs   Cats and Dogs

Underline the nouns in the sentences. **Hint:** There may be more than one or none!

3. <u>Roland</u> is seven <u>years</u> old.

4. Put the <u>book</u> away.

Read each sentence. If it asks a question, put a question mark at the end of the sentence.

5. Who said that?

6. What is your name?

7. Maria is very smart

Add an **e** to each word to make a new word. Write the new word on the lines.

8. bit <u>bite</u>

9. tub <u>tube</u>

10. kit <u>kite</u>

---

prewrite/brainstorm

Fill in the character planner about a character from a story or one you have made up.

He/she hears:
He/she thinks about:
He/she says:
He/she feels:

He/she likes to:

The brainstorming activity should contain various ideas or words related to the topic.

He/she goes to:

Day #1

draft

Write four sentences about the character. Use ideas from your character planner.

The first draft should contain ideas taken from the brainstorming activity.

Day #2

revise

Read the sentences you wrote. Can you make your sentences clearer? Rewrite each sentence.

The next draft should show improvements in organization and detail of information when compared with the first draft.

Day #3

proofread

It's time to proofread your sentences. Read them one more time. Do you see any capitalization errors? Are all the words spelled correctly? Did you use the correct punctuation and grammar? Use proofreading marks to correct the sentences.

- ☐ ✓ Capitalization Mistakes
- ☐ ✓ Odd Grammar
- ☐ ✓ Punctuation Mistakes
- ☐ ✓ Spelling Mistakes

The final draft should show proofreading marks where needed.

Day #4

Assessment #4

publish

Now it is time to publish your writing. Write your final copy on the lines below.
MAKE SURE it turns out:
- NEAT—Make sure there are no wrinkles, creases, or holes.
- CLEAN—Erase any smudges or dirty spots.
- EASY TO READ—Use your best handwriting and good spacing between words.

The content of writing samples will vary. Check to be sure that students have correctly completed all of the earlier steps in the writing process and have followed instructions for publishing their work. Use rubic on page 5 to assess.

Answer Key

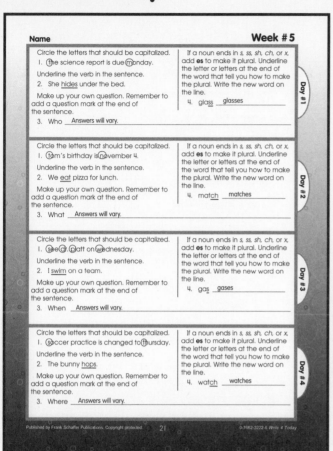

Week # 5

Day #1

Circle the letters that should be capitalized.
1. (T)he science report is due (m)onday.

Underline the verb in the sentence.
2. She <u>hides</u> under the bed.

Make up your own question. Remember to add a question mark at the end of the sentence.
3. Who ___Answers will vary.___

If a noun ends in *s, ss, sh, ch,* or *x,* add **es** to make it plural. Underline the letter or letters at the end of the word that tell you how to make the plural. Write the new word on the line.
4. gla<u>ss</u> ___glasses___

Day #2

Circle the letters that should be capitalized.
1. (T)om's birthday is (n)ovember 4.

Underline the verb in the sentence.
2. We <u>eat</u> pizza for lunch.

Make up your own question. Remember to add a question mark at the end of the sentence.
3. What ___Answers will vary.___

If a noun ends in *s, ss, sh, ch,* or *x,* add **es** to make it plural. Underline the letter or letters at the end of the word that tell you how to make the plural. Write the new word on the line.
4. mat<u>ch</u> ___matches___

Day #3

Circle the letters that should be capitalized.
1. (I) see (d)r. (p)latt on (w)ednesday.

Underline the verb in the sentence.
2. I <u>swim</u> on a team.

Make up your own question. Remember to add a question mark at the end of the sentence.
3. When ___Answers will vary.___

If a noun ends in *s, ss, sh, ch,* or *x,* add **es** to make it plural. Underline the letter or letters at the end of the word that tell you how to make the plural. Write the new word on the line.
4. ga<u>s</u> ___gases___

Day #4

Circle the letters that should be capitalized.
1. (S)occer practice is changed to (t)hursday.

Underline the verb in the sentence.
2. The bunny <u>hops</u>.

Make up your own question. Remember to add a question mark at the end of the sentence.
3. Where ___Answers will vary.___

If a noun ends in *s, ss, sh, ch,* or *x,* add **es** to make it plural. Underline the letter or letters at the end of the word that tell you how to make the plural. Write the new word on the line.
4. wat<u>ch</u> ___watches___

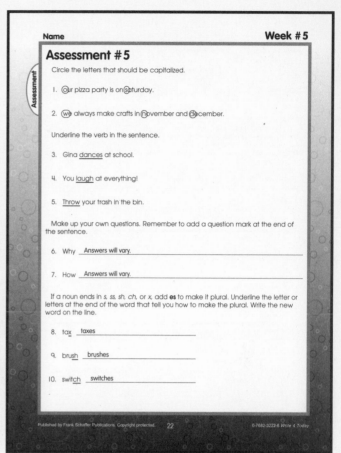

Week # 5

Assessment

Assessment # 5

Circle the letters that should be capitalized.

1. (O)ur pizza party is on (S)aturday.

2. (W)e always make crafts in (n)ovember and (d)ecember.

Underline the verb in the sentence.

3. Gina <u>dances</u> at school.

4. You <u>laugh</u> at everything!

5. <u>Throw</u> your trash in the bin.

Make up your own questions. Remember to add a question mark at the end of the sentence.

6. Why ___Answers will vary.___

7. How ___Answers will vary.___

If a noun ends in *s, ss, sh, ch,* or *x,* add **es** to make it plural. Underline the letter or letters at the end of the word that tell you how to make the plural. Write the new word on the line.

8. ta<u>x</u> ___taxes___

9. bru<u>sh</u> ___brushes___

10. swit<u>ch</u> ___switches___

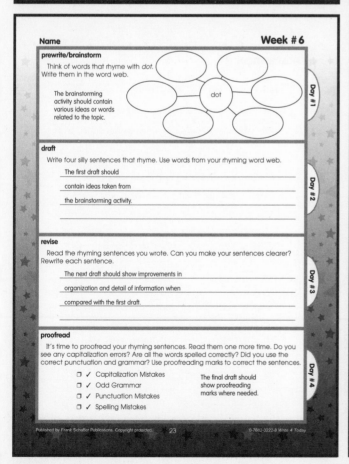

Week # 6

Day #1

prewrite/brainstorm

Think of words that rhyme with *dot.* Write them in the word web.

The brainstorming activity should contain various ideas or words related to the topic.

[dot]

Day #2

draft

Write four silly sentences that rhyme. Use words from your rhyming word web.

___The first draft should___
___contain ideas taken from___
___the brainstorming activity.___

Day #3

revise

Read the rhyming sentences you wrote. Can you make your sentences clearer? Rewrite each sentence.

___The next draft should show improvements in___
___organization and detail of information when___
___compared with the first draft.___

Day #4

proofread

It's time to proofread your rhyming sentences. Read them one more time. Do you see any capitalization errors? Are all the words spelled correctly? Did you use the correct punctuation and grammar? Use proofreading marks to correct the sentences.

☐ ✓ Capitalization Mistakes
☐ ✓ Odd Grammar
☐ ✓ Punctuation Mistakes
☐ ✓ Spelling Mistakes

The final draft should show proofreading marks where needed.

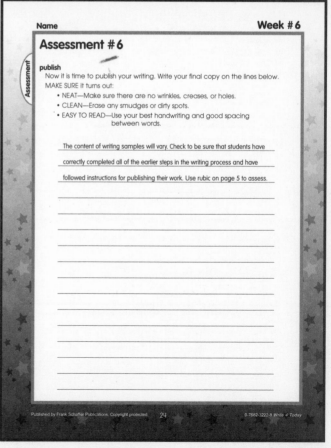

Week # 6

Assessment

Assessment # 6

publish

Now it is time to publish your writing. Write your final copy on the lines below. MAKE SURE it turns out:
- NEAT—Make sure there are no wrinkles, creases, or holes.
- CLEAN—Erase any smudges or dirty spots.
- EASY TO READ—Use your best handwriting and good spacing between words.

___The content of writing samples will vary. Check to be sure that students have___
___correctly completed all of the earlier steps in the writing process and have___
___followed instructions for publishing their work. Use rubic on page 5 to assess.___

Answer Key

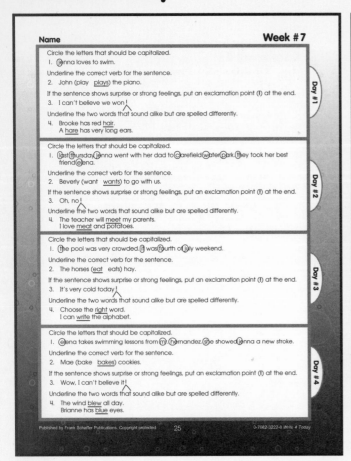

Day #1

Circle the letters that should be capitalized.
1. Jenna loves to swim.
Underline the correct verb for the sentence.
2. John (play __plays__) the piano.
If the sentence shows surprise or strong feelings, put an exclamation point (!) at the end.
3. I can't believe we won !
Underline the two words that sound alike but are spelled differently.
4. Brooke has red __hair__.
A __hare__ has very long ears.

Day #2

Circle the letters that should be capitalized.
1. __L__ast __T__hursday __J__enna went with her dad to __C__arefield __W__ater __P__ark. __T__hey took her best friend __E__lena.
Underline the correct verb for the sentence.
2. Beverly (want __wants__) to go with us.
If the sentence shows surprise or strong feelings, put an exclamation point (!) at the end.
3. Oh, no !
Underline the two words that sound alike but are spelled differently.
4. The teacher will __meet__ my parents.
I love __meat__ and potatoes.

Day #3

Circle the letters that should be capitalized.
1. __T__he pool was very crowded. __I__t was __F__ourth of __J__uly weekend.
Underline the correct verb for the sentence.
2. The horses (eat __eats__) hay.
If the sentence shows surprise or strong feelings, put an exclamation point (!) at the end.
3. It's very cold today !
Underline the two words that sound alike but are spelled differently.
4. Choose the __right__ word.
I can __write__ the alphabet.

Day #4

Circle the letters that should be capitalized.
1. __E__lena takes swimming lessons from __M__r. __H__ernandez. __S__he showed __J__enna a new stroke.
Underline the correct verb for the sentence.
2. Mae (bake __bakes__) cookies.
If the sentence shows surprise or strong feelings, put an exclamation point (!) at the end.
3. Wow, I can't believe it !
Underline the two words that sound alike but are spelled differently.
4. The wind __blew__ all day.
Brianne has __blue__ eyes.

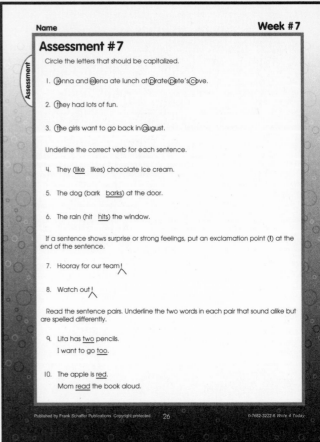

Assessment

Assessment #7

Circle the letters that should be capitalized.

1. __J__enna and __E__lena ate lunch at __P__irate __P__ete's __C__ove.

2. __T__hey had lots of fun.

3. __T__he girls want to go back in __A__ugust.

Underline the correct verb for each sentence.

4. They (__like__ likes) chocolate ice cream.

5. The dog (bark __barks__) at the door.

6. The rain (hit __hits__) the window.

If a sentence shows surprise or strong feelings, put an exclamation point (!) at the end of the sentence.

7. Hooray for our team !

8. Watch out !

Read the sentence pairs. Underline the two words in each pair that sound alike but are spelled differently.

9. Lita has __two__ pencils.
I want to go __too__.

10. The apple is __red__.
Mom __read__ the book aloud.

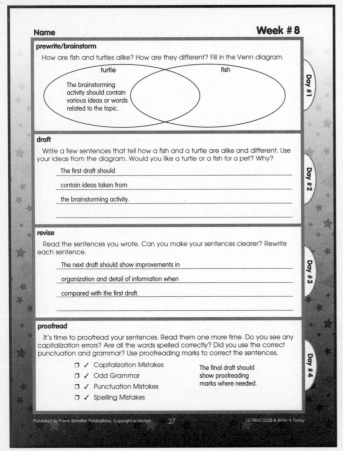

prewrite/brainstorm

How are fish and turtles alike? How are they different? Fill in the Venn diagram.

turtle   fish

The brainstorming activity should contain various ideas or words related to the topic.

Day #1

draft

Write a few sentences that tell how a fish and a turtle are alike and different. Use your ideas from the diagram. Would you like a turtle or a fish for a pet? Why?

The first draft should contain ideas taken from the brainstorming activity.

Day #2

revise

Read the sentences you wrote. Can you make your sentences clearer? Rewrite each sentence.

The next draft should show improvements in organization and detail of information when compared with the first draft.

Day #3

proofread

It's time to proofread your sentences. Read them one more time. Do you see any capitalization errors? Are all the words spelled correctly? Did you use the correct punctuation and grammar? Use proofreading marks to correct the sentences.

☐ ✓ Capitalization Mistakes
☐ ✓ Odd Grammar
☐ ✓ Punctuation Mistakes
☐ ✓ Spelling Mistakes

The final draft should show proofreading marks where needed.

Day #4

Assessment

Assessment #8

publish

Now it is time to publish your writing. Write your final copy on the lines below. MAKE SURE it turns out:
- NEAT—Make sure there are no wrinkles, creases, or holes.
- CLEAN—Erase any smudges or dirty spots.
- EASY TO READ—Use your best handwriting and good spacing between words.

The content of writing samples will vary. Check to be sure that students have correctly completed all of the earlier steps in the writing process and have followed instructions for publishing their work. Use rubic on page 5 to assess.

Answer Key

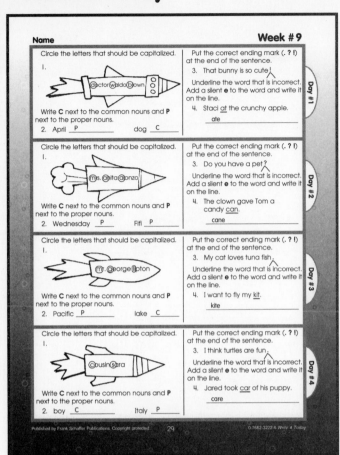

Day #1

Circle the letters that should be capitalized.
1.

(doctor)(waldo)(brown)

Write **C** next to the common nouns and **P** next to the proper nouns.
2. April _P_   dog _C_

Put the correct ending mark (. **?** !) at the end of the sentence.
3. That bunny is so cute!

Underline the word that is incorrect. Add a silent **e** to the word and write it on the line.
4. Staci <u>at</u> the crunchy apple.
ate

Day #2

Circle the letters that should be capitalized.
1.

(mrs.)(anita)(alonzo)

Write **C** next to the common nouns and **P** next to the proper nouns.
2. Wednesday _P_   Fifi _P_

Put the correct ending mark (. **?** !) at the end of the sentence.
3. Do you have a pet?

Underline the word that is incorrect. Add a silent **e** to the word and write it on the line.
4. The clown gave Tom a candy <u>can</u>.
cane

Day #3

Circle the letters that should be capitalized.
1.

(mr.)(george)(upton)

Write **C** next to the common nouns and **P** next to the proper nouns.
2. Pacific _P_   lake _C_

Put the correct ending mark (. **?** !) at the end of the sentence.
3. My cat loves tuna fish.

Underline the word that is incorrect. Add a silent **e** to the word and write it on the line.
4. I want to fly my <u>kit</u>.
kite

Day #4

Circle the letters that should be capitalized.
1.

(cousin)(sara)

Write **C** next to the common nouns and **P** next to the proper nouns.
2. boy _C_   Italy _P_

Put the correct ending mark (. **?** !) at the end of the sentence.
3. I think turtles are fun.

Underline the word that is incorrect. Add a silent **e** to the word and write it on the line.
4. Jared took <u>car</u> of his puppy.
care

Assessment

Assessment #9

Circle the letters that should be capitalized.

1.

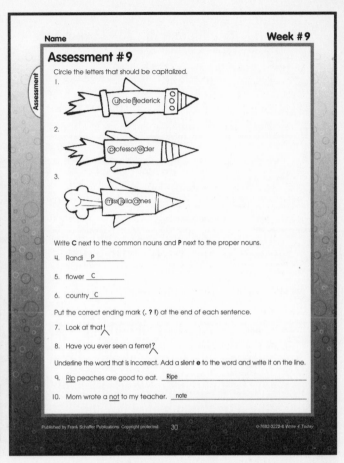

(uncle)(frederick)

2.

(professor)(elder)

3.

(miss)(julia)(ames)

Write **C** next to the common nouns and **P** next to the proper nouns.

4. Randi _P_

5. flower _C_

6. country _C_

Put the correct ending mark (. **?** !) at the end of each sentence.

7. Look at that!

8. Have you ever seen a ferret?

Underline the word that is incorrect. Add a silent **e** to the word and write it on the line.

9. <u>Rip</u> peaches are good to eat. _Ripe_

10. Mom wrote a <u>not</u> to my teacher. _note_

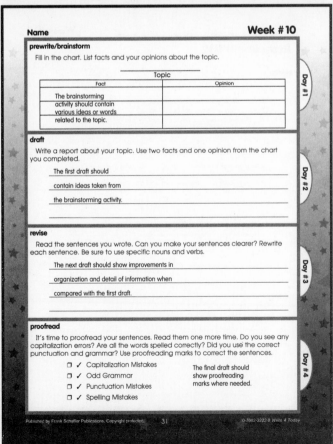

Day #1

prewrite/brainstorm

Fill in the chart. List facts and your opinions about the topic.

Topic	
Fact	Opinion
The brainstorming activity should contain various ideas or words related to the topic.	

Day #2

draft

Write a report about your topic. Use two facts and one opinion from the chart you completed.

The first draft should contain ideas taken from the brainstorming activity.

Day #3

revise

Read the sentences you wrote. Can you make your sentences clearer? Rewrite each sentence. Be sure to use specific nouns and verbs.

The next draft should show improvements in organization and detail of information when compared with the first draft.

Day #4

proofread

It's time to proofread your sentences. Read them one more time. Do you see any capitalization errors? Are all the words spelled correctly? Did you use the correct punctuation and grammar? Use proofreading marks to correct the sentences.

☐ ✓ Capitalization Mistakes
☐ ✓ Odd Grammar
☐ ✓ Punctuation Mistakes
☐ ✓ Spelling Mistakes

The final draft should show proofreading marks where needed.

Assessment

Assessment #10

publish

Now it is time to publish your writing. Write your final copy on the lines below.
MAKE SURE it turns out:

- NEAT—Make sure there are no wrinkles, creases, or holes.
- CLEAN—Erase any smudges or dirty spots.
- EASY TO READ—Use your best handwriting and good spacing between words.

The content of writing samples will vary. Check to be sure that students have correctly completed all of the earlier steps in the writing process and have followed instructions for publishing their work. Use rubic on page 5 to assess.

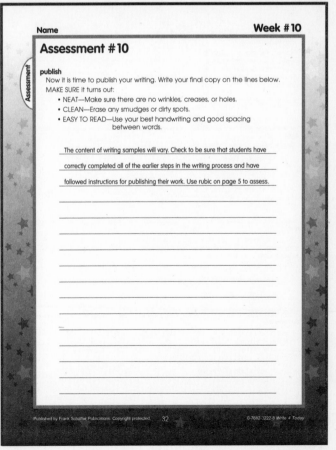

Answer Key

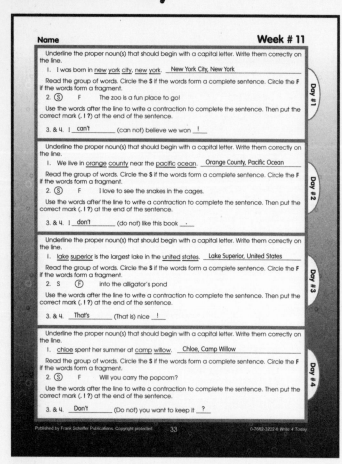

Week # 11

Name

Underline the proper noun(s) that should begin with a capital letter. Write them correctly on the line.
1. I was born in <u>new york city</u>, <u>new york</u>. New York City, New York

Read the group of words. Circle the **S** if the words form a complete sentence. Circle the **F** if the words form a fragment.
2. ⓈF The zoo is a fun place to go!

Use the words after the line to write a contraction to complete the sentence. Then put the correct mark (. ! ?) at the end of the sentence.
3. & 4. I __can't__ (can not) believe we won __!__

Day #1

Underline the proper noun(s) that should begin with a capital letter. Write them correctly on the line.
1. We live in <u>orange county</u> near the <u>pacific ocean</u>. Orange County, Pacific Ocean

Read the group of words. Circle the **S** if the words form a complete sentence. Circle the **F** if the words form a fragment.
2. ⓈF I love to see the snakes in the cages.

Use the words after the line to write a contraction to complete the sentence. Then put the correct mark (. ! ?) at the end of the sentence.
3. & 4. I __don't__ (do not) like this book __.__

Day #2

Underline the proper noun(s) that should begin with a capital letter. Write them correctly on the line.
1. <u>lake superior</u> is the largest lake in the <u>united states</u>. Lake Superior, United States

Read the group of words. Circle the **S** if the words form a complete sentence. Circle the **F** if the words form a fragment.
2. S Ⓕ into the alligator's pond

Use the words after the line to write a contraction to complete the sentence. Then put the correct mark (. ! ?) at the end of the sentence.
3. & 4. __That's__ (That is) nice __!__

Day #3

Underline the proper noun(s) that should begin with a capital letter. Write them correctly on the line.
1. <u>chloe</u> spent her summer at <u>camp willow</u>. Chloe, Camp Willow

Read the group of words. Circle the **S** if the words form a complete sentence. Circle the **F** if the words form a fragment.
2. ⓈF Will you carry the popcorn?

Use the words after the line to write a contraction to complete the sentence. Then put the correct mark (. ! ?) at the end of the sentence.
3. & 4. __Don't__ (Do not) you want to keep it __?__

Day #4

Week #11

Name

Assessment

Assessment #11

Underline the proper noun(s) that should begin with a capital letter. Write them correctly on the lines.

1. <u>ted</u> went to <u>illinois</u> and visited <u>chicago</u>. Ted, Illinois, Chicago

2. <u>bermuda</u> is a country in the <u>atlantic ocean</u>. Bermuda, Atlantic Ocean

3. The capital of <u>michigan</u> is <u>lansing</u>. Michigan, Lansing

Read the groups of words. Circle the **S** if the words form a complete sentence. Circle the **F** if the words form a fragment.

4. S Ⓕ the tall zookeeper
5. ⓈF The lions are sleeping in the sun.
6. ⓈF That seal splashed me!

Put the correct ending mark (. ! ?) at the end of the sentences.

7. Wow, it's just what I wanted !

8. Why is this so cold?

Read the sentences. Use the words under each line to write a contraction to complete the sentences.

9. I __don't__ think we will see Logan at the track meet.
   (do not)

10. Ryan says __that's__ his bike.
    (that is)

Week #12

Name

prewrite/brainstorm

Sometimes you write about a chain of events. Think about a chain of events. Fill in the chart. List every event. List them in the order they happen. If you need more room, write them on another paper. The brainstorming activity should contain various ideas or words related to the topic.

Topic
First,
Next,
Then,
Next,
Then,
Finally,

Day #1

draft

Read your list of events. Write a paragraph that contains all of the events.

The first draft should contain ideas taken from the brainstorming activity.

Day #2

revise

Read the paragraph you wrote. Did you put the events in the order they happened? Can you make your sentences clearer? Rewrite the paragraph. Be sure to use specific nouns and verbs.

The next draft should show improvements in organization and detail of information when compared with the first draft.

Day #3

proofread

It's time to proofread your paragraph. Read it one more time. Do you see any capitalization errors? Are all the words spelled correctly? Did you use the correct punctuation and grammar? Use proofreading marks to correct the sentences.

☐ ✓ Capitalization Mistakes
☐ ✓ Odd Grammar
☐ ✓ Punctuation Mistakes
☐ ✓ Spelling Mistakes

The final draft should show proofreading marks where needed.

Day #4

Week #12

Name

Assessment

Assessment #12

publish

Now it is time to publish your writing. Write your final copy on the lines below. MAKE SURE it turns out:
• NEAT—Make sure there are no wrinkles, creases, or holes.
• CLEAN—Erase any smudges or dirty spots.
• EASY TO READ—Use your best handwriting and good spacing between words.

The content of writing samples will vary. Check to be sure that students have correctly completed all of the earlier steps in the writing process and have followed instructions for publishing their work. Use rubic on page 5 to assess.

Answer Key

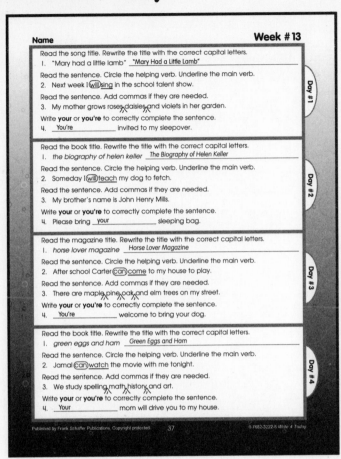

Day #1

Read the song title. Rewrite the title with the correct capital letters.
1. "Mary had a little lamb" _"Mary Had a Little Lamb"_

Read the sentence. Circle the helping verb. Underline the main verb.
2. Next week I (will) sing in the school talent show.

Read the sentence. Add commas if they are needed.
3. My mother grows roses, daisies, and violets in her garden.

Write **your** or **you're** to correctly complete the sentence.
4. _You're_ invited to my sleepover.

Day #2

Read the book title. Rewrite the title with the correct capital letters.
1. the biography of helen keller _The Biography of Helen Keller_

Read the sentence. Circle the helping verb. Underline the main verb.
2. Someday I (will) teach my dog to fetch.

Read the sentence. Add commas if they are needed.
3. My brother's name is John Henry Mills.

Write **your** or **you're** to correctly complete the sentence.
4. Please bring _your_ sleeping bag.

Day #3

Read the magazine title. Rewrite the title with the correct capital letters.
1. horse lover magazine _Horse Lover Magazine_

Read the sentence. Circle the helping verb. Underline the main verb.
2. After school Carter (can) come to my house to play.

Read the sentence. Add commas if they are needed.
3. There are maple, pine, oak, and elm trees on my street.

Write **your** or **you're** to correctly complete the sentence.
4. _You're_ welcome to bring your dog.

Day #4

Read the book title. Rewrite the title with the correct capital letters.
1. green eggs and ham _Green Eggs and Ham_

Read the sentence. Circle the helping verb. Underline the main verb.
2. Jamal (can) watch the movie with me tonight.

Read the sentence. Add commas if they are needed.
3. We study spelling, math, history, and art.

Write **your** or **you're** to correctly complete the sentence.
4. _Your_ mom will drive you to my house.

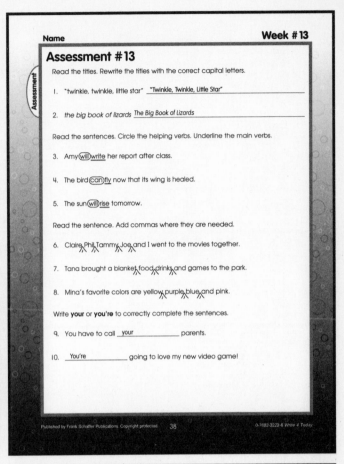

Assessment

Assessment #13

Read the titles. Rewrite the titles with the correct capital letters.

1. "twinkle, twinkle, little star" _"Twinkle, Twinkle, Little Star"_

2. the big book of lizards _The Big Book of Lizards_

Read the sentences. Circle the helping verbs. Underline the main verbs.

3. Amy (will) write her report after class.

4. The bird (can) fly now that its wing is healed.

5. The sun (will) rise tomorrow.

Read the sentence. Add commas where they are needed.

6. Claire, Phil, Tammy, Joe, and I went to the movies together.

7. Tana brought a blanket, food, drinks, and games to the park.

8. Mina's favorite colors are yellow, purple, blue, and pink.

Write **your** or **you're** to correctly complete the sentences.

9. You have to call _your_ parents.

10. _You're_ going to love my new video game!

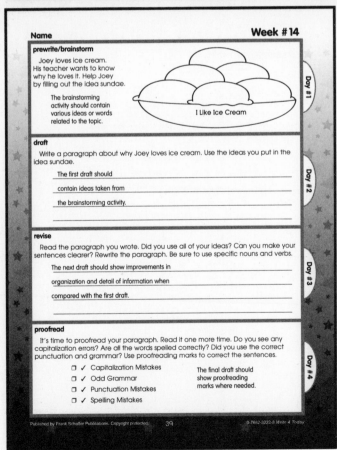

Day #1

prewrite/brainstorm
Joey loves ice cream. His teacher wants to know why he loves it. Help Joey by filling out the idea sundae.

The brainstorming activity should contain various ideas or words related to the topic.

I Like Ice Cream

Day #2

draft
Write a paragraph about why Joey loves ice cream. Use the ideas you put in the idea sundae.

The first draft should contain ideas taken from the brainstorming activity.

Day #3

revise
Read the paragraph you wrote. Did you use all of your ideas? Can you make your sentences clearer? Rewrite the paragraph. Be sure to use specific nouns and verbs.

The next draft should show improvements in organization and detail of information when compared with the first draft.

Day #4

proofread
It's time to proofread your paragraph. Read it one more time. Do you see any capitalization errors? Are all the words spelled correctly? Did you use the correct punctuation and grammar? Use proofreading marks to correct the sentences.

☐ ✓ Capitalization Mistakes
☐ ✓ Odd Grammar
☐ ✓ Punctuation Mistakes
☐ ✓ Spelling Mistakes

The final draft should show proofreading marks where needed.

Assessment

Assessment #14

publish
Now it is time to publish your writing. Write your final copy on the lines below. MAKE SURE it turns out:
- NEAT—Make sure there are no wrinkles, creases, or holes.
- CLEAN—Erase any smudges or dirty spots.
- EASY TO READ—Use your best handwriting and good spacing between words.

The content of writing samples will vary. Check to be sure that students have correctly completed all of the earlier steps in the writing process and have followed instructions for publishing their work. Use rubic on page 5 to assess.

Answer Key

Circle the correct verb. Use proofreading marks to show the correct capital letters.

1. & 2. my team (goes) go) to soccer practice on tuesdays and thursdays.

Read the sentence. Add apostrophes where they are needed.

3. Jamals grass is thick and green.

Look at the picture. Circle the correct plural noun.

4. 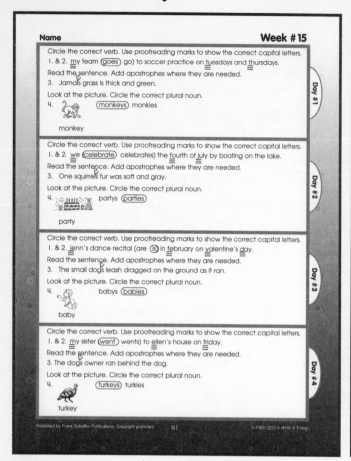 (monkeys) monkies

monkey

Day #1

Circle the correct verb. Use proofreading marks to show the correct capital letters.

1. & 2. we (celebrate) celebrates) the fourth of july by boating on the lake.

Read the sentence. Add apostrophes where they are needed.

3. One squirrels fur was soft and gray.

Look at the picture. Circle the correct plural noun.

4. partys (parties)

party

Day #2

Circle the correct verb. Use proofreading marks to show the correct capital letters.

1. & 2. jenn's dance recital (are (is) in february on valentine's day.

Read the sentence. Add apostrophes where they are needed.

3. The small dogs leash dragged on the ground as it ran.

Look at the picture. Circle the correct plural noun.

4. babys (babies)

baby

Day #3

Circle the correct verb. Use proofreading marks to show the correct capital letters.

1. & 2. my sister (went) wents) to ellen's house on friday.

Read the sentence. Add apostrophes where they are needed.

3. The dogs owner ran behind the dog.

Look at the picture. Circle the correct plural noun.

4. (turkeys) turkies

turkey

Day #4

Assessment #15

Assessment

Use proofreading marks to show the correct capital letters.

1. my sister will be six years old in may.

2. In january, we always go sledding on saturday mornings.

3. Jamie's favorite holiday is hanukkah, which comes in december.

Circle the correct verb that completes each sentence.

4. Our team (wear (wears) red uniforms.

5. My grandparents (live) lives) next door.

Read the sentences. Add apostrophes where they are needed.

6. Jamies favorite dessert is ice cream.

7. The mother birds nest was made of mud and twigs.

8. My dads car is dark green.

Look at each picture. Circle the correct plural noun.

9. 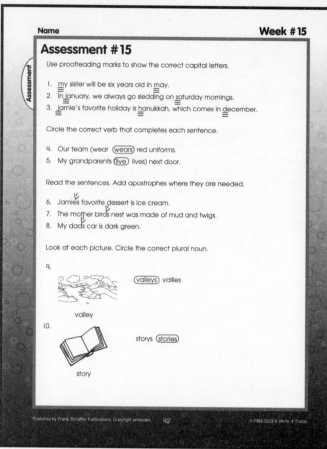 (valleys) vallies

valley

10. storys (stories)

story

---

prewrite/brainstorm

Look at the picture.
What are the kids doing?
Fill in the chart with the
five Ws about the picture.

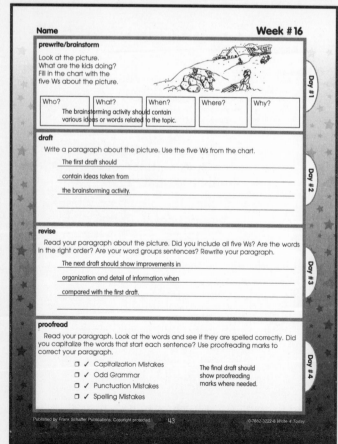

Who?	What?	When?	Where?	Why?
	The brainstorming activity should contain various ideas or words related to the topic.			

Day #1

draft

Write a paragraph about the picture. Use the five Ws from the chart.

The first draft should

contain ideas taken from

the brainstorming activity.

Day #2

revise

Read your paragraph about the picture. Did you include all five Ws? Are the words in the right order? Are your word groups sentences? Rewrite your paragraph.

The next draft should show improvements in

organization and detail of information when

compared with the first draft.

Day #3

proofread

Read your paragraph. Look at the words and see if they are spelled correctly. Did you capitalize the words that start each sentence? Use proofreading marks to correct your paragraph.

- ☐ ✓ Capitalization Mistakes
- ☐ ✓ Odd Grammar
- ☐ ✓ Punctuation Mistakes
- ☐ ✓ Spelling Mistakes

The final draft should
show proofreading
marks where needed.

Day #4

Assessment #16

Assessment

publish

Now it is time to publish your writing. Write your final copy on the lines below. MAKE SURE it turns out:

- NEAT—Make sure there are no wrinkles, creases, or holes.
- CLEAN—Erase any smudges or dirty spots.
- EASY TO READ—Use your best handwriting and good spacing between words.

The content of writing samples will vary. Check to be sure that students have

correctly completed all of the earlier steps in the writing process and have

followed instructions for publishing their work. Use rubic on page 5 to assess.

Answer Key

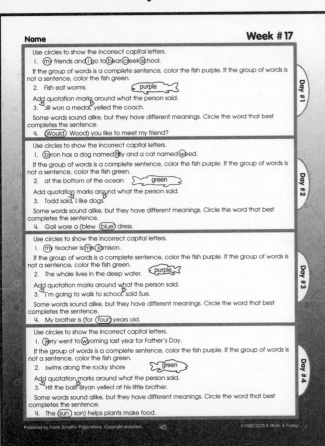

Use circles to show the incorrect capital letters.
1. (m)y friends and (I) go to (b)ear (c)reek (s)chool.

If the group of words is a complete sentence, color the fish purple. If the group of words is not a sentence, color the fish green.
2. Fish eat worms.   purple

Add quotation marks around what the person said.
3. "Jill won a medal," yelled the coach.

Some words sound alike, but they have different meanings. Circle the word that best completes the sentence.
4. (Would) Wood) you like to meet my friend?

Day #1

Use circles to show the incorrect capital letters.
1. (b)yron has a dog named (l)illy and a cat named (w)eed.

If the group of words is a complete sentence, color the fish purple. If the group of words is not a sentence, color the fish green.
2. at the bottom of the ocean   green

Add quotation marks around what the person said.
3. Todd said, I like dogs.

Some words sound alike, but they have different meanings. Circle the word that best completes the sentence.
4. Gail wore a (blew (blue) dress.

Day #2

Use circles to show the incorrect capital letters.
1. (m)y teacher is (m)rs. (j)amison.

If the group of words is a complete sentence, color the fish purple. If the group of words is not a sentence, color the fish green.
2. The whale lives in the deep water.   purple

Add quotation marks around what the person said.
3. I'm going to walk to school," said Sue.

Some words sound alike, but they have different meanings. Circle the word that best completes the sentence.
4. My brother is (for (four) years old.

Day #3

Use circles to show the incorrect capital letters.
1. (j)erry went to (w)yoming last year for Father's Day.

If the group of words is a complete sentence, color the fish purple. If the group of words is not a sentence, color the fish green.
2. swims along the rocky shore   green

Add quotation marks around what the person said.
3. Hit the ball," Bryan yelled at his little brother.

Some words sound alike, but they have different meanings. Circle the word that best completes the sentence.
4. The (sun) son) helps plants make food.

Day #4

Assessment

Assessment #17

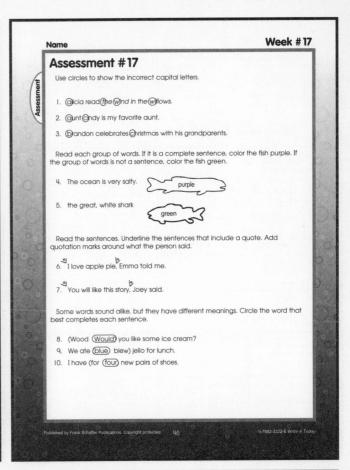

Use circles to show the incorrect capital letters.

1. (a)licia read (t)he (w)ind in the (w)illows.

2. (a)unt (c)indy is my favorite aunt.

3. (b)randon celebrates (c)hristmas with his grandparents.

Read each group of words. If it is a complete sentence, color the fish purple. If the group of words is not a sentence, color the fish green.

4. The ocean is very salty.   purple

5. the great, white shark   green

Read the sentences. Underline the sentences that include a quote. Add quotation marks around what the person said.

6. "I love apple pie," Emma told me.

7. "You will like this story," Joey said.

Some words sound alike, but they have different meanings. Circle the word that best completes each sentence.

8. (Wood (Would) you like some ice cream?

9. We ate (blue) blew) jello for lunch.

10. I have (for (four) new pairs of shoes.

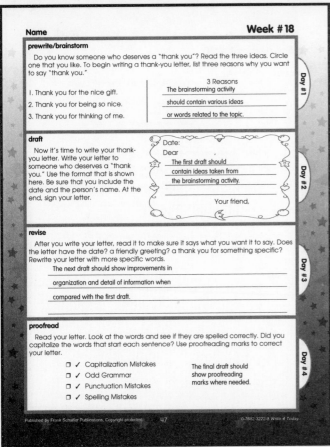

prewrite/brainstorm

Do you know someone who deserves a "thank you"? Read the three ideas. Circle one that you like. To begin writing a thank-you letter, list three reasons why you want to say "thank you."

1. Thank you for the nice gift.

2. Thank you for being so nice.

3. Thank you for thinking of me.

3 Reasons
The brainstorming activity
should contain various ideas
or words related to the topic.

Day #1

draft

Now it's time to write your thank-you letter. Write your letter to someone who deserves a "thank you." Use the format that is shown here. Be sure that you include the date and the person's name. At the end, sign your letter.

Date:
Dear
The first draft should
contain ideas taken from
the brainstorming activity.
Your friend,

Day #2

revise

After you write your letter, read it to make sure it says what you want it to say. Does the letter have the date? a friendly greeting? a thank you for something specific? Rewrite your letter with more specific words.

The next draft should show improvements in
organization and detail of information when
compared with the first draft.

Day #3

proofread

Read your letter. Look at the words and see if they are spelled correctly. Did you capitalize the words that start each sentence? Use proofreading marks to correct your letter.

☐ ✓ Capitalization Mistakes
☐ ✓ Odd Grammar
☐ ✓ Punctuation Mistakes
☐ ✓ Spelling Mistakes

The final draft should
show proofreading
marks where needed.

Day #4

Assessment

Assessment #18

publish

Now it is time to publish your writing. Write your final copy on the lines below. MAKE SURE it turns out:
- **NEAT**—Make sure there are no wrinkles, creases, or holes.
- **CLEAN**—Erase any smudges or dirty spots.
- **EASY TO READ**—Use your best handwriting and good spacing between words.

The content of writing samples will vary. Check to be sure that students have
correctly completed all of the earlier steps in the writing process and have
followed instructions for publishing their work. Use rubic on page 5 to assess.

Answer Key

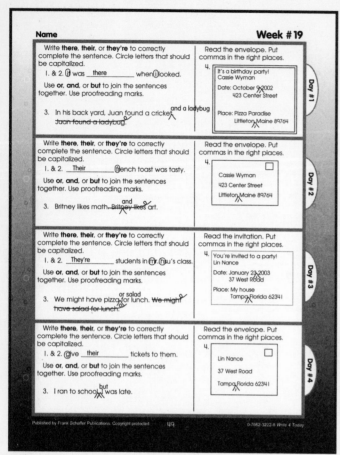

Write **there**, **their**, or **they're** to correctly complete the sentence. Circle letters that should be capitalized.

1. & 2. ⓘt was ___there___ when ⓘ looked.

Use **or**, **and**, or **but** to join the sentences together. Use proofreading marks.

3. In his back yard, Juan found a cricket ^and a ladybug. ~~Juan found a ladybug.~~

Read the envelope. Put commas in the right places.

4.
It's a birthday party!
Cassie Wyman
Date: October 9, 2002
423 Center Street
Place: Pizza Paradise
Littleton, Maine 89764

Write **there**, **their**, or **they're** to correctly complete the sentence. Circle letters that should be capitalized.

1. & 2. ___Their___ ⓕrench toast was tasty.

Use **or**, **and**, or **but** to join the sentences together. Use proofreading marks.

3. Britney likes math. ^and ~~Britney likes art.~~

Read the envelope. Put commas in the right places.

4.
Cassie Wyman
423 Center Street
Littleton, Maine 89764

Write **there**, **their**, or **they're** to correctly complete the sentence. Circle letters that should be capitalized.

1. & 2. ___They're___ students in ⓜr. ⓗsu's class.

Use **or**, **and**, or **but** to join the sentences together. Use proofreading marks.

3. We might have pizza for lunch. ^or salad ~~We might have salad for lunch.~~

Read the invitation. Put commas in the right places.

4.
You're invited to a party!
Lin Nance
Date: January 23, 2003
37 West Road
Place: My house
Tampa, Florida 62341

Write **there**, **their**, or **they're** to correctly complete the sentence. Circle letters that should be capitalized.

1. & 2. ⓖive ___their___ tickets to them.

Use **or**, **and**, or **but** to join the sentences together. Use proofreading marks.

3. I ran to school ^but ~~I~~ was late.

Read the envelope. Put commas in the right places.

4.
Lin Nance
37 West Road
Tampa, Florida 62341

Day #1 / Day #2 / Day #3 / Day #4

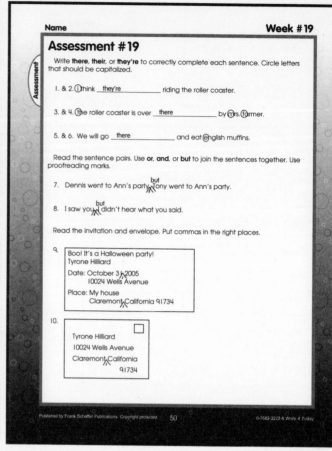

Assessment #19

Write **there**, **their**, or **they're** to correctly complete each sentence. Circle letters that should be capitalized.

1. & 2. ⓘ think ___they're___ riding the roller coaster.

3. & 4. ⓣhe roller coaster is over ___there___ by ⓜrs. ⓕarmer.

5. & 6. We will go ___there___ and eat ⓔnglish muffins.

Read the sentence pairs. Use **or**, **and**, or **but** to join the sentences together. Use proofreading marks.

7. Dennis went to Ann's party. ^but ~~Tony~~ went to Ann's party.

8. I saw you ^but ~~I~~ didn't hear what you said.

Read the invitation and envelope. Put commas in the right places.

9.
Boo! It's a Halloween party!
Tyrone Hilliard
Date: October 31, 2005
10024 Wells Avenue
Place: My house
Claremont, California 91734

10.
Tyrone Hilliard
10024 Wells Avenue
Claremont, California
91734

Assessment

---

prewrite/brainstorm

Some people write stories about their lives. You can, too! Fill in the lines to begin your autobiography.

My name is ___The brainstorming___

My favorite toy is ___activity should contain___

My favorite color is ___various ideas or words___

I like to eat ___related to the topic.___

My friends are _____

draft

Put your sentences in a paragraph. Make sure you put things in the order you want them to be said.

___The first draft should___

___contain ideas taken from___

___the brainstorming activity.___

revise

Read your paragraph about yourself. Did you use all of your ideas? Can you make your sentences clearer? Rewrite the paragraph. Be sure to use specific nouns and verbs.

___The next draft should show improvements in___

___organization and detail of information when___

___compared with the first draft.___

proofread

Read your paragraph. Look at the words and see if they are spelled correctly. Did you capitalize the words that start each sentence? Use proofreading marks to correct your paragraph.

☐ ✓ Capitalization Mistakes
☐ ✓ Odd Grammar
☐ ✓ Punctuation Mistakes
☐ ✓ Spelling Mistakes

The final draft should show proofreading marks where needed.

Day #1 / Day #2 / Day #3 / Day #4

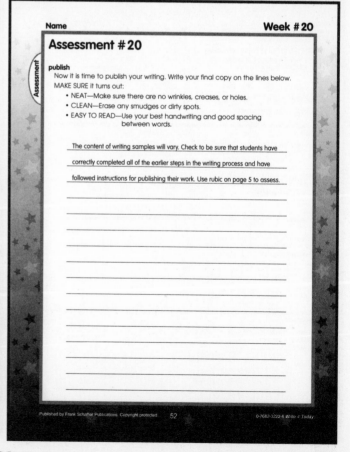

Assessment #20

publish

Now it is time to publish your writing. Write your final copy on the lines below. MAKE SURE it turns out:

- NEAT—Make sure there are no wrinkles, creases, or holes.
- CLEAN—Erase any smudges or dirty spots.
- EASY TO READ—Use your best handwriting and good spacing between words.

___The content of writing samples will vary. Check to be sure that students have___

___correctly completed all of the earlier steps in the writing process and have___

___followed instructions for publishing their work. Use rubic on page 5 to assess.___

Assessment

Answer Key

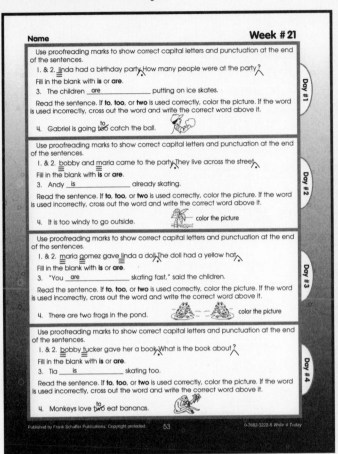

Day #1

Use proofreading marks to show correct capital letters and punctuation at the end of the sentences.

1. & 2. linda had a birthday party How many people were at the party?

Fill in the blank with **is** or **are**.

3. The children _are_ putting on ice skates.

Read the sentence. If **to**, **too**, or **two** is used correctly, color the picture. If the word is used incorrectly, cross out the word and write the correct word above it.

4. Gabriel is going too catch the ball. *(to)*

Day #2

Use proofreading marks to show correct capital letters and punctuation at the end of the sentences.

1. & 2. bobby and maria came to the party They live across the street.

Fill in the blank with **is** or **are**.

3. Andy _is_ already skating.

Read the sentence. If **to**, **too**, or **two** is used correctly, color the picture. If the word is used incorrectly, cross out the word and write the correct word above it.

4. It is too windy to go outside.   color the picture

Day #3

Use proofreading marks to show correct capital letters and punctuation at the end of the sentences.

1. & 2. maria gomez gave linda a doll The doll had a yellow hat.

Fill in the blank with **is** or **are**.

3. "You _are_ skating fast," said the children.

Read the sentence. If **to**, **too**, or **two** is used correctly, color the picture. If the word is used incorrectly, cross out the word and write the correct word above it.

4. There are two frogs in the pond.   color the picture

Day #4

Use proofreading marks to show correct capital letters and punctuation at the end of the sentences.

1. & 2. bobby tucker gave her a book What is the book about?

Fill in the blank with **is** or **are**.

3. Tia _is_ skating too.

Read the sentence. If **to**, **too**, or **two** is used correctly, color the picture. If the word is used incorrectly, cross out the word and write the correct word above it.

4. Monkeys love two eat bananas. *(to)*

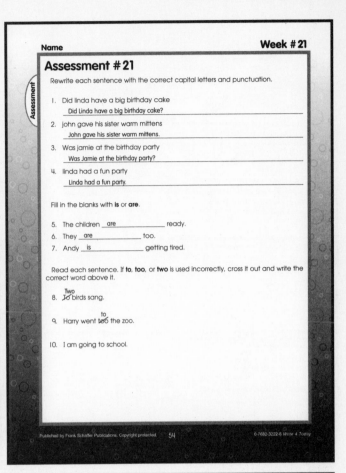

Assessment

Assessment # 21

Rewrite each sentence with the correct capital letters and punctuation.

1. Did linda have a big birthday cake
   Did Linda have a big birthday cake?

2. john gave his sister warm mittens
   John gave his sister warm mittens.

3. Was jamie at the birthday party
   Was Jamie at the birthday party?

4. linda had a fun party
   Linda had a fun party.

Fill in the blanks with **is** or **are**.

5. The children _are_ ready.

6. They _are_ too.

7. Andy _is_ getting tired.

Read each sentence. If **to**, **too**, or **two** is used incorrectly, cross it out and write the correct word above it.

8. To birds sang. *(Two)*

9. Harry went too the zoo. *(to)*

10. I am going to school.

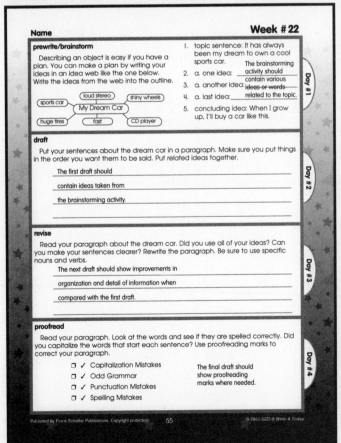

prewrite/brainstorm

Describing an object is easy if you have a plan. You can make a plan by writing your ideas in an idea web like the one below. Write the ideas from the web into the outline.

loud stereo   shiny wheels
sports car   My Dream Car
huge tires   fast   CD player

Day #1

1. topic sentence: It has always been my dream to own a cool sports car.
2. a. one idea: _____
3. a. another idea: _____
4. a. last idea: _____

The brainstorming activity should contain various ideas or words related to the topic.

5. concluding idea: When I grow up, I'll buy a car like this.

draft

Put your sentences about the dream car in a paragraph. Make sure you put things in the order you want them to be said. Put related ideas together.

The first draft should contain ideas taken from the brainstorming activity.

Day #2

revise

Read your paragraph about the dream car. Did you use all of your ideas? Can you make your sentences clearer? Rewrite the paragraph. Be sure to use specific nouns and verbs.

The next draft should show improvements in organization and detail of information when compared with the first draft.

Day #3

proofread

Read your paragraph. Look at the words and see if they are spelled correctly. Did you capitalize the words that start each sentence? Use proofreading marks to correct your paragraph.

- ☐ ✓ Capitalization Mistakes
- ☐ ✓ Odd Grammar
- ☐ ✓ Punctuation Mistakes
- ☐ ✓ Spelling Mistakes

The final draft should show proofreading marks where needed.

Day #4

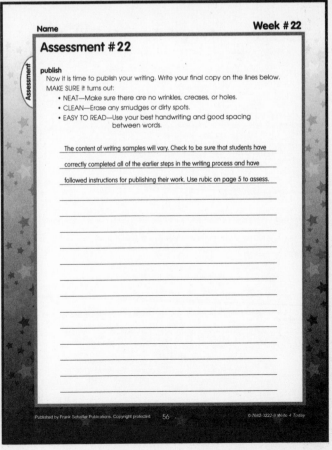

Assessment

Assessment # 22

publish

Now it is time to publish your writing. Write your final copy on the lines below. MAKE SURE it turns out:

- NEAT—Make sure there are no wrinkles, creases, or holes.
- CLEAN—Erase any smudges or dirty spots.
- EASY TO READ—Use your best handwriting and good spacing between words.

The content of writing samples will vary. Check to be sure that students have correctly completed all of the earlier steps in the writing process and have followed instructions for publishing their work. Use rubic on page 5 to assess.

Answer Key

Name

Week # 23

Fill in the blank with the correct contraction.
1. "We __aren't__ going to paint now," said the teacher. (isn't, aren't)

Put quotation marks around the words the person said. Use proofreading marks to show capital letters.
2. & 3. ~Karen~ rode her bike on ~walnut street~. I'm bored, she said.

Read each noun. Write its plural.
4. rose __roses__   bee __bees__

Day #1

Fill in the blank with the correct contraction.
1. The children __weren't__ happy. (wasn't, weren't)

Put quotation marks around the words the person said. Use proofreading marks to show capital letters.
2. & 3. She visited ~nancy~ on ~central boulevard~. Nancy said, Let's meet ~keisha~.

Read each noun. Write its plural.
4. poppy __poppies__   fly __flies__

Day #2

Fill in the blank with the correct contraction.
1. "You __aren't__ going to paint because you are going to the park," said the teacher. (isn't, aren't)

Put quotation marks around the words the person said. Use proofreading marks to show capital letters.
2. & 3. ~Karen~ and ~nancy~ rode to ~garden avenue~. Shall we play at our school? asked ~Keisha~.

Read each noun. Write its plural.
4. bag __bags__   poem __poems__

Day #3

Fill in the blank with the correct contraction.
1. The park __isn't__ crowded today. (isn't, aren't)

Put quotation marks around the words the person said. Use proofreading marks to show capital letters.
2. & 3. They rode to their school on ~cherry road~. Let's race! yelled the girls.

Read each noun. Write its plural.
4. box __boxes__   wish __wishes__

Day #4

Published by Frank Schaffer Publications. Copyright protected.   57   0-7682-3222-8 *Write 4 Today*

Name

Week # 23

Assessment # 23

Assessment

Fill in the blanks with the correct contraction.

1. Amy still __wasn't__ happy. (wasn't, weren't)

2. "Why __weren't__ you happy, Amy?" asked the teacher. (wasn't, weren't)

3. "I am unhappy because we __aren't__ going to paint now," said Amy. (isn't, aren't)

Rewrite each sentence. Begin the names of streets with capital letters.

4. They passed apple road on their way.
   __They passed Apple Road on their way.__

5. Karen, Nancy, and Keisha crossed seventh street.
   __Karen, Nancy, and Keisha crossed Seventh Street.__

Put quotation marks around the words each person said. **Hint:** Periods, commas, question marks, and exclamation points go inside quotation marks.

6. Did you read that book? asked Luisa.

7. Yes, said Becca. Did you?

Read each noun. Write its plural.

8. whale __whales__   tree __trees__

9. penny __pennies__   sky __skies__

10. fox __foxes__   bush __bushes__

Published by Frank Schaffer Publications. Copyright protected.   58   0-7682-3222-8 *Write 4 Today*

Name

Week # 24

prewrite/brainstorm

Brainstorming is a way to think of all kinds of writing ideas. You might use some ideas. You might throw some out. Answer the questions below about your family.
How many people are in your family? _____
What are their names? _____
Write two words that tell about each person in your family. _____
_____
Do you have any pets? _____
What is your family's favorite thing to do together? _____

The brainstorming activity should contain various ideas or words related to the topic.

Day #1

draft

Use your answers to write five sentences about your family. Make sure you put things in the order you want them to be said. Put related ideas together.
__The first draft should__
__contain ideas taken from__
__the brainstorming activity.__
_____

Day #2

revise

Read your five sentences about your family. Do you want to change the order? Can you make your sentences clearer? Rewrite the sentences. Be sure to use specific nouns and verbs.
__The next draft should show improvements in__
__organization and detail of information when__
__compared with the first draft.__

Day #3

proofread

Read your sentences about your family. Look at the words and see if they are spelled correctly. Did you capitalize the words that start each sentence? Use proofreading marks to correct your sentences.
☐ ✓ Capitalization Mistakes
☐ ✓ Odd Grammar
☐ ✓ Punctuation Mistakes
☐ ✓ Spelling Mistakes

The final draft should show proofreading marks where needed.

Day #4

Published by Frank Schaffer Publications. Copyright protected.   59   0-7682-3222-8 *Write 4 Today*

Name

Week # 24

Assessment # 24

Assessment

publish

Now it is time to publish your writing. Write your final copy on the lines below. MAKE SURE it turns out:
- NEAT—Make sure there are no wrinkles, creases, or holes.
- CLEAN—Erase any smudges or dirty spots.
- EASY TO READ—Use your best handwriting and good spacing between words.

__The content of writing samples will vary. Check to be sure that students have__
__correctly completed all of the earlier steps in the writing process and have__
__followed instructions for publishing their work. Use rubic on page 5 to assess.__

Published by Frank Schaffer Publications. Copyright protected.   60   0-7682-3222-8 *Write 4 Today*

Answer Key

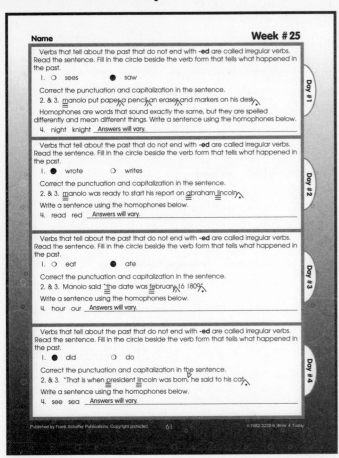

Verbs that tell about the past that do not end with **-ed** are called irregular verbs. Read the sentence. Fill in the circle beside the verb form that tells what happened in the past.

I. ○ sees   ● saw

Correct the punctuation and capitalization in the sentence.

2. & 3. manolo put paper, a pencil, an eraser, and markers on his desk.

Homophones are words that sound exactly the same, but they are spelled differently and mean different things. Write a sentence using the homophones below.

4. night knight _Answers will vary._

Day #1

Verbs that tell about the past that do not end with **-ed** are called irregular verbs. Read the sentence. Fill in the circle beside the verb form that tells what happened in the past.

I. ● wrote   ○ writes

Correct the punctuation and capitalization in the sentence.

2. & 3. manolo was ready to start his report on abraham lincoln.

Write a sentence using the homophones below.

4. read red _Answers will vary._

Day #2

Verbs that tell about the past that do not end with **-ed** are called irregular verbs. Read the sentence. Fill in the circle beside the verb form that tells what happened in the past.

I. ○ eat   ● ate

Correct the punctuation and capitalization in the sentence.

2. & 3. Manolo said "the date was february 16 1809."

Write a sentence using the homophones below.

4. hour our _Answers will vary._

Day #3

Verbs that tell about the past that do not end with **-ed** are called irregular verbs. Read the sentence. Fill in the circle beside the verb form that tells what happened in the past.

I. ● did   ○ do

Correct the punctuation and capitalization in the sentence.

2. & 3. "That is when president lincoln was born," he said to his cat.

Write a sentence using the homophones below.

4. see sea _Answers will vary._

Day #4

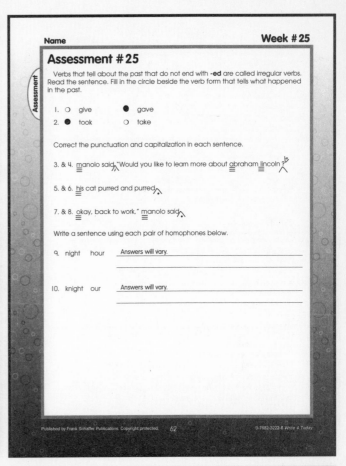

Assessment # 25

Assessment

Verbs that tell about the past that do not end with **-ed** are called irregular verbs. Read the sentence. Fill in the circle beside the verb form that tells what happened in the past.

I. ○ give   ● gave

2. ● took   ○ take

Correct the punctuation and capitalization in each sentence.

3. & 4. manolo said, "Would you like to learn more about abraham lincoln?"

5. & 6. his cat purred and purred.

7. & 8. okay, back to work," manolo said.

Write a sentence using each pair of homophones below.

9. night hour _Answers will vary._

10. knight our _Answers will vary._

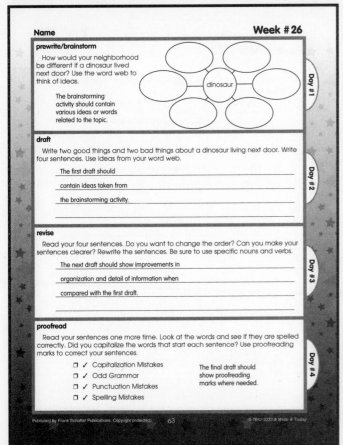

prewrite/brainstorm

How would your neighborhood be different if a dinosaur lived next door? Use the word web to think of ideas.

The brainstorming activity should contain various ideas or words related to the topic.

dinosaur

Day #1

draft

Write two good things and two bad things about a dinosaur living next door. Write four sentences. Use ideas from your word web.

The first draft should contain ideas taken from the brainstorming activity.

Day #2

revise

Read your four sentences. Do you want to change the order? Can you make your sentences clearer? Rewrite the sentences. Be sure to use specific nouns and verbs.

The next draft should show improvements in organization and detail of information when compared with the first draft.

Day #3

proofread

Read your sentences one more time. Look at the words and see if they are spelled correctly. Did you capitalize the words that start each sentence? Use proofreading marks to correct your sentences.

☐ ✓ Capitalization Mistakes
☐ ✓ Odd Grammar
☐ ✓ Punctuation Mistakes
☐ ✓ Spelling Mistakes

The final draft should show proofreading marks where needed.

Day #4

Assessment # 26

Assessment

publish

Now it is time to publish your writing. Write your final copy on the lines below. MAKE SURE it turns out:

- NEAT—Make sure there are no wrinkles, creases, or holes.
- CLEAN—Erase any smudges or dirty spots.
- EASY TO READ—Use your best handwriting and good spacing between words.

The content of writing samples will vary. Check to be sure that students have correctly completed all of the earlier steps in the writing process and have followed instructions for publishing their work. Use rubic on page 5 to assess.

Answer Key

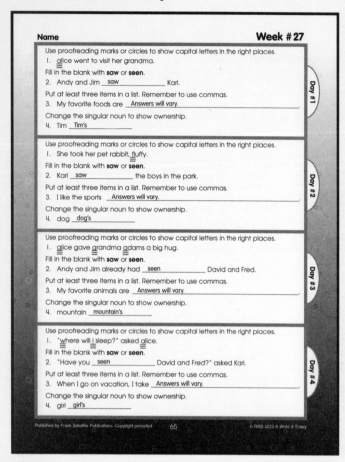

Use proofreading marks or circles to show capital letters in the right places.
1. alice went to visit her grandma.

Fill in the blank with **saw** or **seen**.
2. Andy and Jim __saw__ Karl.

Put at least three items in a list. Remember to use commas.
3. My favorite foods are __Answers will vary.__

Change the singular noun to show ownership.
4. Tim __Tim's__

Day #1

Use proofreading marks or circles to show capital letters in the right places.
1. She took her pet rabbit, fluffy.

Fill in the blank with **saw** or **seen**.
2. Karl __saw__ the boys in the park.

Put at least three items in a list. Remember to use commas.
3. I like the sports __Answers will vary.__

Change the singular noun to show ownership.
4. dog __dog's__

Day #2

Use proofreading marks or circles to show capital letters in the right places.
1. alice gave grandma adams a big hug.

Fill in the blank with **saw** or **seen**.
2. Andy and Jim already had __seen__ David and Fred.

Put at least three items in a list. Remember to use commas.
3. My favorite animals are __Answers will vary.__

Change the singular noun to show ownership.
4. mountain __mountain's__

Day #3

Use proofreading marks or circles to show capital letters in the right places.
1. "where will i sleep?" asked alice.

Fill in the blank with **saw** or **seen**.
2. "Have you __seen__ David and Fred?" asked Karl.

Put at least three items in a list. Remember to use commas.
3. When I go on vacation, I take __Answers will vary.__

Change the singular noun to show ownership.
4. girl __girl's__

Day #4

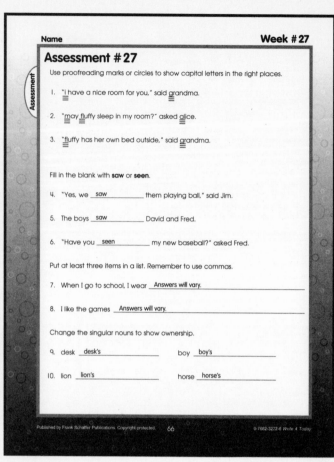

Assessment # 27

Use proofreading marks or circles to show capital letters in the right places.

1. "i have a nice room for you," said grandma.

2. "may fluffy sleep in my room?" asked alice.

3. "fluffy has her own bed outside," said grandma.

Fill in the blank with **saw** or **seen**.

4. "Yes, we __saw__ them playing ball," said Jim.

5. The boys __saw__ David and Fred.

6. "Have you __seen__ my new baseball?" asked Fred.

Put at least three items in a list. Remember to use commas.

7. When I go to school, I wear __Answers will vary.__

8. I like the games __Answers will vary.__

Change the singular nouns to show ownership.

9. desk __desk's__   boy __boy's__

10. lion __lion's__   horse __horse's__

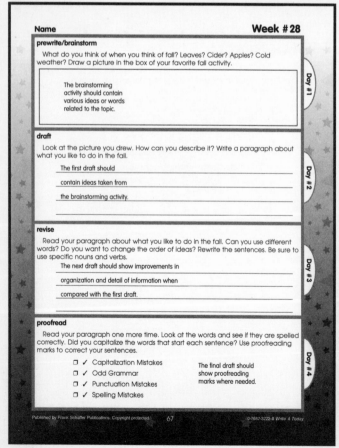

prewrite/brainstorm

What do you think of when you think of fall? Leaves? Cider? Apples? Cold weather? Draw a picture in the box of your favorite fall activity.

> The brainstorming activity should contain various ideas or words related to the topic.

Day #1

draft

Look at the picture you drew. How can you describe it? Write a paragraph about what you like to do in the fall.

> The first draft should
> contain ideas taken from
> the brainstorming activity.

Day #2

revise

Read your paragraph about what you like to do in the fall. Can you use different words? Do you want to change the order of ideas? Rewrite the sentences. Be sure to use specific nouns and verbs.

> The next draft should show improvements in
> organization and detail of information when
> compared with the first draft.

Day #3

proofread

Read your paragraph one more time. Look at the words and see if they are spelled correctly. Did you capitalize the words that start each sentence? Use proofreading marks to correct your sentences.

☐ ✓ Capitalization Mistakes
☐ ✓ Odd Grammar
☐ ✓ Punctuation Mistakes
☐ ✓ Spelling Mistakes

> The final draft should
> show proofreading
> marks where needed.

Day #4

Assessment # 28

publish

Now it is time to publish your writing. Write your final copy on the lines below. MAKE SURE it turns out:
- NEAT—Make sure there are no wrinkles, creases, or holes.
- CLEAN—Erase any smudges or dirty spots.
- EASY TO READ—Use your best handwriting and good spacing between words.

> The content of writing samples will vary. Check to be sure that students have
> correctly completed all of the earlier steps in the writing process and have
> followed instructions for publishing their work. Use rubic on page 5 to assess.

Answer Key

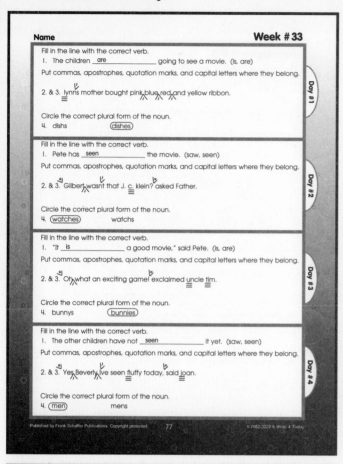

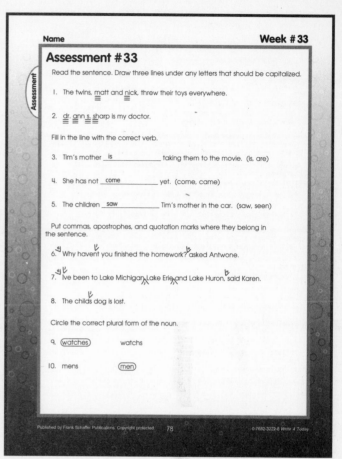

Fill in the line with the correct verb.
1. The children **are** going to see a movie. (is, are)

Put commas, apostrophes, quotation marks, and capital letters where they belong.

2. & 3. lynns mother bought pink, blue, red, and yellow ribbon.

Circle the correct plural form of the noun.
4. dishs   (dishes)

Fill in the line with the correct verb.
1. Pete has **seen** the movie. (saw, seen)

Put commas, apostrophes, quotation marks, and capital letters where they belong.

2. & 3. Gilbert, wasn't that J. c. klein? asked Father.

Circle the correct plural form of the noun.
4. (watches)   watchs

Fill in the line with the correct verb.
1. "It **is** a good movie," said Pete. (is, are)

Put commas, apostrophes, quotation marks, and capital letters where they belong.

2. & 3. Oh, what an exciting game! exclaimed uncle tim.

Circle the correct plural form of the noun.
4. bunnys   (bunnies)

Fill in the line with the correct verb.
1. The other children have not **seen** it yet. (saw, seen)

Put commas, apostrophes, quotation marks, and capital letters where they belong.

2. & 3. Yes, Beverly, I've seen fluffy today, said joan.

Circle the correct plural form of the noun.
4. (men)   mens

Day #1 / Day #2 / Day #3 / Day #4

Assessment # 33

Read the sentence. Draw three lines under any letters that should be capitalized.

1. The twins, matt and nick, threw their toys everywhere.

2. dr. ann s. sharp is my doctor.

Fill in the line with the correct verb.

3. Tim's mother **is** taking them to the movie. (is, are)

4. She has not **come** yet. (come, came)

5. The children **saw** Tim's mother in the car. (saw, seen)

Put commas, apostrophes, and quotation marks where they belong in the sentence.

6. Why haven't you finished the homework? asked Antwone.

7. I've been to Lake Michigan, Lake Erie, and Lake Huron, said Karen.

8. The child's dog is lost.

Circle the correct plural form of the noun.

9. (watches)   watchs

10. mens   (men)

---

prewrite/brainstorm

A concluding sentence comes at the end of a paragraph. It tells the main idea in a different way, or it gives the reader something to think about. What is your favorite book? In the oval, write the title of your favorite book. On the three lines next to it, write three supporting ideas about why you like the book.

The brainstorming activity
should contain various ideas
or words related to the topic.

draft

Write a topic sentence about why you like your favorite book. Write three sentences supporting why you like the book. Now write a concluding sentence that tells your main idea in a different way.

The first draft should
contain ideas taken from
the brainstorming activity.

revise

Read your paragraph. Did you name the book? Did you begin with a topic sentence? Did you write three supporting sentences to explain your main idea? Does your concluding statement tell your main idea in a different way? Rewrite your paragraph.

The next draft should show improvements in
organization and detail of information when
compared with the first draft.

proofread

Read your paragraph one more time. Look at the words and see if they are spelled correctly. Did you capitalize the words that should start with a capital letter? Is the punctuation correct? Use proofreading marks to correct your paragraph.

☐ ✓ Capitalization Mistakes
☐ ✓ Odd Grammar
☐ ✓ Punctuation Mistakes
☐ ✓ Spelling Mistakes

The final draft should show proofreading marks where needed.

Day #1 / Day #2 / Day #3 / Day #4

Assessment # 34

publish

Now it is time to publish your writing. Write your final copy on the lines below. MAKE SURE it turns out:
- NEAT—Make sure there are no wrinkles, creases, or holes.
- CLEAN—Erase any smudges or dirty spots.
- EASY TO READ—Use your best handwriting and good spacing between words.

The content of writing samples will vary. Check to be sure that students have
correctly completed all of the earlier steps in the writing process and have
followed instructions for publishing their work. Use rubic on page 5 to assess.

Answer Key

Name

Week #35

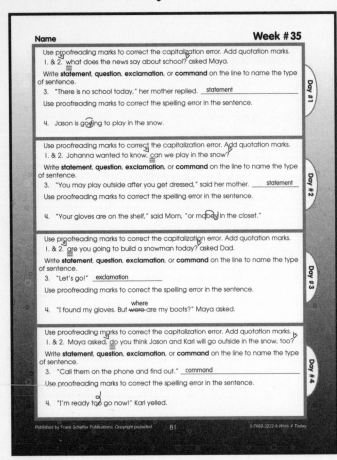

Use proofreading marks to correct the capitalization error. Add quotation marks.
1. & 2. what does the news say about school? asked Maya.

Write **statement**, **question**, **exclamation**, or **command** on the line to name the type of sentence.

3. "There is no school today," her mother replied. ___statement___

Use proofreading marks to correct the spelling error in the sentence.

4. Jason is going to play in the snow.

Day #1

Use proofreading marks to correct the capitalization error. Add quotation marks.
1. & 2. Johanna wanted to know, can we play in the snow?

Write **statement**, **question**, **exclamation**, or **command** on the line to name the type of sentence.

3. "You may play outside after you get dressed," said her mother. ___statement___

Use proofreading marks to correct the spelling error in the sentence.

4. "Your gloves are on the shelf," said Mom, "or maybe in the closet."

Day #2

Use proofreading marks to correct the capitalization error. Add quotation marks.
1. & 2. are you going to build a snowman today? asked Dad.

Write **statement**, **question**, **exclamation**, or **command** on the line to name the type of sentence.

3. "Let's go!" ___exclamation___

Use proofreading marks to correct the spelling error in the sentence.

4. "I found my gloves. But where are my boots?" Maya asked.

Day #3

Use proofreading marks to correct the capitalization error. Add quotation marks.
1. & 2. Maya asked, do you think Jason and Karl will go outside in the snow, too?

Write **statement**, **question**, **exclamation**, or **command** on the line to name the type of sentence.

3. "Call them on the phone and find out." ___command___

Use proofreading marks to correct the spelling error in the sentence.

4. "I'm ready to go now!" Karl yelled.

Day #4

Name

Week #35

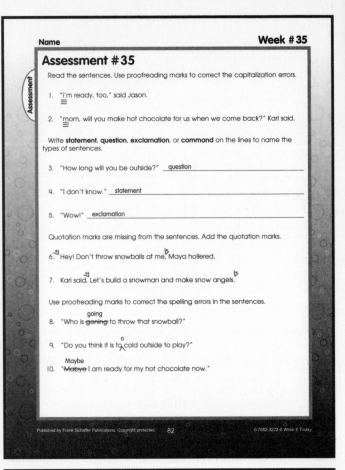

Assessment

Assessment #35

Read the sentences. Use proofreading marks to correct the capitalization errors.

1. "i'm ready, too," said Jason.

2. "mom, will you make hot chocolate for us when we come back?" Karl said.

Write **statement**, **question**, **exclamation**, or **command** on the lines to name the types of sentences.

3. "How long will you be outside?" ___question___

4. "I don't know." ___statement___

5. "Wow!" ___exclamation___

Quotation marks are missing from the sentences. Add the quotation marks.

6. Hey! Don't throw snowballs at me, Maya hollered.

7. Karl said, Let's build a snowman and make snow angels.

Use proofreading marks to correct the spelling errors in the sentences.

8. "Who is going to throw that snowball?"

9. "Do you think it is to cold outside to play?"

10. "Mabye I am ready for my hot chocolate now." _(correction: Maybe)_

Name

Week #36

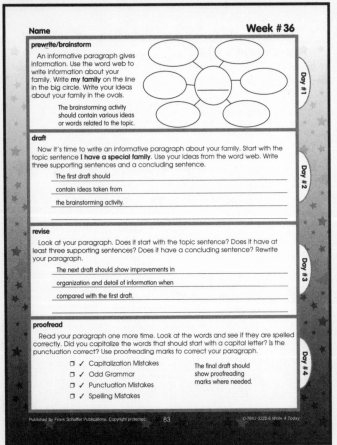

prewrite/brainstorm

An informative paragraph gives information. Use the word web to write information about your family. Write **my family** on the line in the big circle. Write your ideas about your family in the ovals.

The brainstorming activity should contain various ideas or words related to the topic.

Day #1

draft

Now it's time to write an informative paragraph about your family. Start with the topic sentence **I have a special family**. Use your ideas from the word web. Write three supporting sentences and a concluding sentence.

The first draft should contain ideas taken from the brainstorming activity.

Day #2

revise

Look at your paragraph. Does it start with the topic sentence? Does it have at least three supporting sentences? Does it have a concluding sentence? Rewrite your paragraph.

The next draft should show improvements in organization and detail of information when compared with the first draft.

Day #3

proofread

Read your paragraph one more time. Look at the words and see if they are spelled correctly. Did you capitalize the words that should start with a capital letter? Is the punctuation correct? Use proofreading marks to correct your paragraph.

- ✓ Capitalization Mistakes
- ✓ Odd Grammar
- ✓ Punctuation Mistakes
- ✓ Spelling Mistakes

The final draft should show proofreading marks where needed.

Day #4

Name

Week #36

Assessment

Assessment #36

publish

Now it is time to publish your writing. Write your final copy on the lines below.
MAKE SURE it turns out:
- NEAT—Make sure there are no wrinkles, creases, or holes.
- CLEAN—Erase any smudges or dirty spots.
- EASY TO READ—Use your best handwriting and good spacing between words.

The content of writing samples will vary. Check to be sure that students have correctly completed all of the earlier steps in the writing process and have followed instructions for publishing their work. Use rubic on page 5 to assess.

Answer Key

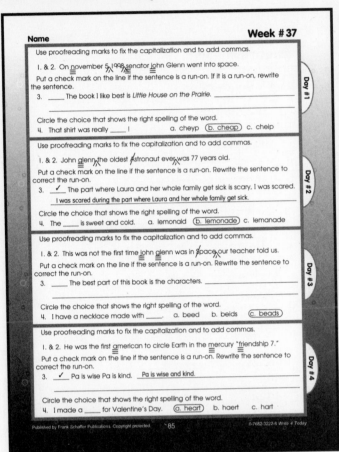
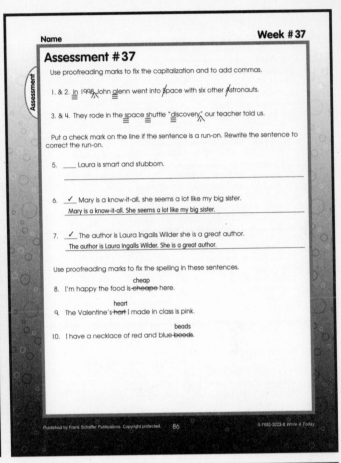

Week #37

Use proofreading marks to fix the capitalization and to add commas.

1. & 2. On november 5, 1998 senator john Glenn went into space.

Put a check mark on the line if the sentence is a run-on. If it is a run-on, rewrite the sentence.

3. _____ The book I like best is *Little House on the Prairie*. _____

Circle the choice that shows the right spelling of the word.

4. That shirt was really _____ !   a. cheyp   (b. cheap)   c. cieph

Day #1

Use proofreading marks to fix the capitalization and to add commas.

1. & 2. John glenn, the oldest astronaut ever, was 77 years old.

Put a check mark on the line if the sentence is a run-on. Rewrite the sentence to correct the run-on.

3. ✓ The part where Laura and her whole family get sick is scary, I was scared.
I was scared during the part where Laura and her whole family get sick.

Circle the choice that shows the right spelling of the word.

4. The _____ is sweet and cold.   a. lemonald   (b. lemonade)   c. lemanade

Day #2

Use proofreading marks to fix the capitalization and to add commas.

1. & 2. This was not the first time john glenn was in space, our teacher told us.

Put a check mark on the line if the sentence is a run-on. Rewrite the sentence to correct the run-on.

3. _____ The best part of this book is the characters. _____

Circle the choice that shows the right spelling of the word.

4. I have a necklace made with _____.   a. beed   b. beids   (c. beads)

Day #3

Use proofreading marks to fix the capitalization and to add commas.

1. & 2. He was the first american to circle Earth in the mercury "friendship 7."

Put a check mark on the line if the sentence is a run-on. Rewrite the sentence to correct the run-on.

3. ✓ Pa is wise Pa is kind.   Pa is wise and kind.

Circle the choice that shows the right spelling of the word.

4. I made a _____ for Valentine's Day.   (a. heart)   b. haert   c. hart

Day #4

Assessment #37

Use proofreading marks to fix the capitalization and to add commas.

1. & 2. In 1998, John glenn went into space with six other astronauts.

3. & 4. They rode in the space shuttle "discovery," our teacher told us.

Put a check mark on the line if the sentence is a run-on. Rewrite the sentence to correct the run-on.

5. _____ Laura is smart and stubborn.
_____

6. ✓ Mary is a know-it-all, she seems a lot like my big sister.
Mary is a know-it-all. She seems a lot like my big sister.

7. ✓ The author is Laura Ingalls Wilder she is a great author.
The author is Laura Ingalls Wilder. She is a great author.

Use proofreading marks to fix the spelling in these sentences.

8. I'm happy the food is ~~cheape~~ here.   cheap

9. The Valentine's ~~hart~~ I made in class is pink.   heart

10. I have a necklace of red and blue ~~beeds~~.   beads

prewrite/brainstorm

Narrative writing tells a story that may or may not be true. To plan a story, you use a story map. You need characters, a setting, and a problem. Next, you need events and a solution.

Here are your characters, setting, and problem: You and your best friend are at the beach on Saturday, and you find a bottle with a treasure map inside. You don't know if it's real or not. Write one event and a solution based on this information.

The brainstorming activity should contain various
ideas or words related to the topic.

Day #1

draft

Write a paragraph about you, your friend, and the treasure map you found on the beach. Describe the event that happens after you find the map. Write the solution to the story.

The first draft should
contain ideas taken from
the brainstorming activity.

Day #2

revise

Read your paragraph. Does it tell the story in the right order? Did you introduce your topic? Did you write a solution to the story? Rewrite your paragraph, and make your words more specific.

The next draft should show improvements in
organization and detail of information when
compared with the first draft.

Day #3

proofread

Now it's time to proofread your paragraph. Are all of the words spelled correctly? Did you capitalize words that need to be capitalized? Did you use the correct verbs and nouns? Proofread your paragraph.

☐ ✓ Capitalization Mistakes
☐ ✓ Odd Grammar
☐ ✓ Punctuation Mistakes
☐ ✓ Spelling Mistakes

The final draft should show proofreading marks where needed.

Day #4

Assessment #38

publish

Now it is time to publish your writing. Write your final copy on the lines below. MAKE SURE it turns out:

- NEAT—Make sure there are no wrinkles, creases, or holes.
- CLEAN—Erase any smudges or dirty spots.
- EASY TO READ—Use your best handwriting and good spacing between words.

The content of writing samples will vary. Check to be sure that students have
correctly completed all of the earlier steps in the writing process and have
followed instructions for publishing their work. Use rubic on page 5 to assess.

Answer Key

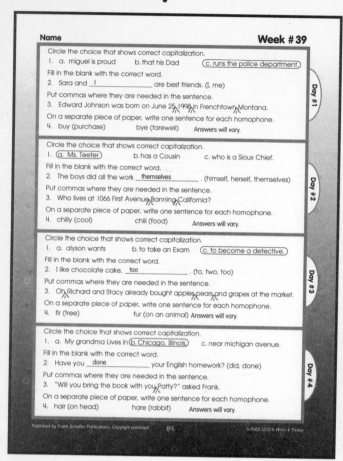

Name — Week #39

Day #1

Circle the choice that shows correct capitalization.
1. a. miguel is proud   b. that his Dad   (c. runs the police department.)

Fill in the blank with the correct word.
2. Sara and _I_ are best friends. (I, me)

Put commas where they are needed in the sentence.
3. Edward Johnson was born on June 25, 1998, in Frenchtown, Montana.

On a separate piece of paper, write one sentence for each homophone.
4. buy (purchase)   bye (farewell)   Answers will vary.

Day #2

Circle the choice that shows correct capitalization.
1. (a. Ms. Teeter)   b. has a Cousin   c. who is a Sioux Chief.

Fill in the blank with the correct word.
2. The boys did all the work _themselves_ . (himself, herself, themselves)

Put commas where they are needed in the sentence.
3. Who lives at 1066 First Avenue, Banning, California?

On a separate piece of paper, write one sentence for each homophone.
4. chilly (cool)   chili (food)   Answers will vary.

Day #3

Circle the choice that shows correct capitalization.
1. a. alyson wants   b. to take an Exam   (c. to become a detective.)

Fill in the blank with the correct word.
2. I like chocolate cake, _too_ . (to, two, too)

Put commas where they are needed in the sentence.
3. Oh, Richard and Stacy already bought apples, pears, and grapes at the market.

On a separate piece of paper, write one sentence for each homophone.
4. fir (tree)   fur (on an animal)   Answers will vary.

Day #4

Circle the choice that shows correct capitalization.
1. a. My grandma Lives in (b. Chicago, Illinois.)   c. near michigan avenue.

Fill in the blank with the correct word.
2. Have you _done_ your English homework? (did, done)

Put commas where they are needed in the sentence.
3. "Will you bring the book with you, Patty?" asked Frank.

On a separate piece of paper, write one sentence for each homophone.
4. hair (on head)   hare (rabbit)   Answers will vary.

Name — Week #39

Assessment #39

Circle the choice that shows correct capitalization.

1. a. The city of pontiac
   b. was named for a Chief
   (c. who lived in Michigan.)

2. a. Mystic, connecticut
   b. is the Town where
   (c. my grandparents live.)

Fill in the blank with the correct word.

3. There are _too_ many children swimming today. (to, two, too)
4. Luisa went to the movies by _herself_ . (himself, herself, themselves)
5. Joey and _I_ ran to the store. (I, me)

Put commas where they are needed in the sentence.

6. "Oh, I forgot the book at school," said Patty.
7. "Can we borrow another book, Frank?" she asked.

Write one sentence for each homophone.

8. road (street)   Answers will vary.
   rode (from ride)   Answers will vary.

9. shoe (covers foot)   Answers will vary.
   shoo (chase away)   Answers will vary.

10. lay (recline)   Answers will vary.
    lei (flower necklace)   Answers will vary.

Name — Week #40

Day #1

prewrite/brainstorm

You have decided to enter the "Take a Family Vacation on Us" contest. To enter you must submit an eight-line poem which explains why your family should win the vacation. Use the idea web to organize your thoughts. You may add more boxes on a separate piece of paper. The brainstorming activity should contain various ideas or words related to the topic.

Take a Vacation on Us Contest

Reasons My Family Deserves to Win

Adjectives That Describe My Family

Day #2

draft

The winning poem must express good reasons for needing the vacation. Write your eight-line poem. Be sure to support your reasons with specific words.

The first draft should contain ideas taken from the brainstorming activity.

Day #3

revise

Read your poem. Does it tell the reasons your family should win the vacation? Did you use good words to describe your reasons? Did you write eight lines? Rewrite your poem, and make your words more specific.

The next draft should show improvements in organization and detail of information when compared with the first draft.

Day #4

proofread

Now it's time to proofread your poem. Are all of the words spelled correctly? Did you capitalize words that need to be capitalized? Did you use the correct verbs and nouns? Use proofreading marks to correct your poem.

☐ ✓ Capitalization Mistakes
☐ ✓ Odd Grammar
☐ ✓ Punctuation Mistakes
☐ ✓ Spelling Mistakes

The final draft should show proofreading marks where needed.

Name — Week #40

Assessment #40

publish

Now it is time to publish your writing. Write your final copy on the lines below. MAKE SURE it turns out:
• NEAT—Make sure there are no wrinkles, creases, or holes.
• CLEAN—Erase any smudges or dirty spots.
• EASY TO READ—Use your best handwriting and good spacing between words.

The content of writing samples will vary. Check to be sure that students have correctly completed all of the earlier steps in the writing process and have followed instructions for publishing their work. Use rubic on page 5 to assess.